Desire and the Divine

SOUTHERN LITERARY STUDIES

FRED HOBSON, *Series Editor*

Desire and the Divine

FEMININE IDENTITY IN
WHITE SOUTHERN WOMEN'S WRITING

Kathaleen E. Amende

LOUISIANA STATE UNIVERSITY PRESS)|(BATON ROUGE

Published by Louisiana State University Press
Copyright © 2013 by Louisiana State University Press
Manufactured in the United States of America
FIRST PRINTING

DESIGNER: *Mandy McDoanld Scallan*
TYPEFACE: *Whitman*
PRINTER: *McNaughton & Gunn, Inc.*
BINDER: *Dekker Bookbinding*

Library of Congress Cataloging-in-Publication Data

Amende, Kathaleen E., 1972–
  Desire and the divine : feminine identity in white southern women's writing / Kathaleen E. Amende.
     pages cm. — (Southern literary studies)
  Includes bibliographical references and index.
  ISBN 978-0-8071-5038-2 (cloth : alk. paper) — ISBN 978-0-8071-5039-9 (pdf) — ISBN 978-0-8071-
5040-5 (epub) — ISBN 978-0-8071-5041-2 (mobi) 1. American fiction—Southern states—History
and criticism. 2. American fiction—Women authors—History and criticism. 3. American fiction—
White authors—History and criticism. 4. Women and literature—Southern States. 5. Women in
literature. 6. Desire in literature. 7. Sex in literature. 8. Religion in literature. I. Title.
  PS261.A54 2013
  810.9'92870975—dc23

                                                                                              2012038753

To my mother, Dorrina F. Amende.
She is my friend, my inspiration, and my hero.

CONTENTS

ACKNOWLEDGMENTS

This book has been the work of many years and has undergone numerous changes and versions. Although it started as a doctoral dissertation, it barely resembles those early drafts. Because of the time span of my life that this project has covered, and because this book, like all others, is the work of more than just a writer, there is no way to acknowledge everyone who has influenced its writing. Still, I am honored and humbled to thank even some of the friends, colleagues, and family who have made this effort possible.

For their support in the earliest stages, I cannot strongly enough thank those who worked with me at Tulane University, especially the committee who reviewed this when it was still a dissertation. Dr. Barry Ahearn and Dr. Felipe Smith provided valuable insights and essential challenges that strengthened not only the arguments but my way of thinking about the core issues. Dr. Rebecca Mark read multiple versions of this text and offered scholarly expertise, wisdom, and friendship, often when I needed it most.

Louisiana State University Press, especially editors John Easterly, Margaret H. Lovecraft, and Lee Sioles have been amazingly wonderful to work with and have made my first manuscript experience an easy and friendly one. Fred Hobson, editor of the Southern Literary Studies series, offered the manuscript a home and provided a reading that helped give me new and confident insights.

I would also like to offer my gratitude to the administrations of both Tulane and Alabama State universities who were generous with resources and funding so that I could travel for research and to conferences where I presented the early versions of the ideas contained in these pages. As well, my colleagues and students at both universities were patient and understanding while I worked to complete the manuscript.

And last, but not least, there is a group of people who have been essential to my life during the completion of this project. I cannot thank these people enough, and merely mentioning them here seems far too meager a thank you, but I hope they know just how valuable they have been to me. My family, especially my mother, Dorrina, and my father, Ernest, have provided unending inspiration and listened to me talk about this project for much longer than I have actually been working on it. I would be a lesser woman without their support and love. Many thanks go out to Gary Richards for being my mentor and friend and providing support in every way from discussing ideas to reading papers to listening to me vent to performing weddings; to Bill Kte'pi for the great conversations on writing and the (perhaps even greater) food; to Lindsey, Alicia, Vic, Robert, Rob, Tiffany, Russ, and Susan for not kicking me out of the group despite all the nights I ditched you all for long hours of writing; to Taylor Lindberg for offering love and emotional support during some rough patches; and, from the very bottom of my heart, to Mark Hill for being the most amazing partner and spouse I could have asked for. Not only did he offer his love and support, as a fellow scholar he provided invaluable support as reader, editor, listener, and philosopher. Never could I have imagined finding someone with whom I could be so perfectly matched. Thank you.

Desire and the Divine

CHAPTER 1

Southern Women, Desire, and the Divine

In an amusingly revealing anecdote, Lee Smith tells interviewer Susan Ketchin that, as a teenager, she would go on dates with her boyfriend to the local church revivals where she would be saved "constantly." She explains that "religion and sex—you know, excitement, passion—were all together. I couldn't differentiate between sexual passion and religious passion. This was what we all did on dates, was go to the revival. It was a turn-on" (45). Such a moment—the moment of passion that is unidentifiable as being either religious or sexual, but clearly resembles both—is what this book is about. The very existence of such a text as Ketchin's *The Christ-Haunted Landscape* is enough to make clear the importance that religion has long held in southern studies and for southerners in general. Southern historian Samuel S. Hill, for example, has spent much of his career writing volumes with titles such as *The Encyclopedia of Religion in the South* and *Southern Churches in Crisis*. To look at the moment where the sacred merges with the secular in a moment of *passion* though—that is something that needs to be explored.

While it is true that such moments occur occasionally in literature from regions outside the South, they occur not only more explicitly, but also with more frequency in late-twentieth-century southern women's literature, particularly in literature by white southern women. The reasons are grounded in the history and culture of the South—a place which has long seen itself as separate from the rest of the country and where conservative nineteenth-century Christian orthodoxy and belief in the ideals of "true womanhood" persisted much longer than they did elsewhere in America. As Samuel Hill and Charles Reagan Wilson have pointed out in numerous works, the South exists as an entity mainly because it chose, after the Civil War, to see itself as a last bastion of hope in a primarily spiritual war that required strict adherence to such nineteenth century ideologies.[1] It thus defined itself as a place that, while unsuccessful at political secession, was definitely its own world racially, religiously, and culturally. This postwar South became a place apart, a world where people held tenaciously to ideals that the average non-southerner would soon give up in the face of late-nineteenth and early twentieth-century modernity and postbellum industrialism.

In such a world, the merging of the secular and the sacred is fairly normalized. If the region's identity is a religious one, then it follows that no part of culture is ever completely separate from religion, and this truth is borne out by the propensity of southerners, both in history and in literature, to turn the secular into the sacred. The "religion of the Lost Cause," for example, while not existing as a "real" religion, has become a site of sacred understanding for generations of southerners. Similarly, where Lee Smith sees the erotic possibilities of a religious revival, the sacred can easily be applied to the secular and, in this case, the sexual. When mergings between the sexual and the sacred do occur in non-southern literature, they tend to happen in communities that are either set apart from the "normal" culture of the time and place, or the people who experience them are considered strange or emphatically "special." In the literature of southern white women, however, particularly those of the late twentieth century, such moments occur both in communities set "apart" *and* in everyday society, and the women who experience such, while occasionally being seen as "chosen" or "special," are more often seen simply as "normal."

The most popular and familiar non-southern texts that deal with such mergings are the hagiographies and writings of the Catholic medieval mystics, most of whom were either cloistered or condemned for their beliefs. Some more modern texts, such as Sinclair Lewis's 1927 *Elmer Gantry* or Ron Hansen's 1992 novel *Mariette in Ecstasy,* similarly present the embrace of a sacred/sexual combination as occurring only to those who are properly removed from society or who suffer from some sort of mental illness. In *Elmer Gantry,* the evangelist Sharon Falconer insists that having sex with Elmer will only "symbolize [her] complete union with Jesus" (173), but will only consent to such an act after properly removing herself to a cloistered home in the country and afterwards insists that any sexual activity be done only in secrecy. In Hansen's novel, Mariette, a nun who communes with Jesus, mortifies her flesh, and suffers stigmata, is both cloistered *and* considered by many to be either insane or pathological. Other texts, such as James Baldwin's 1952 semiautobiographical *Go Tell it on the Mountain* and Eugene O'Neill's 1956 play *Long Day's Journey into Night,* are more rare in that such moments occur in the lives of average people, but even they depict these events only as evidence of abnormality, suffering, or sickness. In contrast, during the last three decades of the twentieth century, southern authors such as Rosemary Daniell and Connie May Fowler present characters who, like the authors themselves, grow up believing that Jesus should be a girl's first "boyfriend." As Lee Smith points out, even using revivals as "turn-ons" was something "we all did."

Given the privileged place of religion in southern culture, it thus makes sense that this merging of the secular and sacred is prevalent not just in literature about adults, but also in literature about girls who are in their most sexually formative years. This is the merging, for example, that Rosemary Daniell describes in her autobiography when she, as a young teenager, sits in church, alternately staring at her boyfriend and studying the stained-glass Jesus, imagining that "what I feel . . . when Troy holds my hands as we roller-skate, becomes, as I bow my head, a vision of myself raised high, safe, warm in a blond savior's arms" (102). This is also this moment Florida writer Sheri Reynolds shows us when Ninah Huff, the teenage protagonist of *Rapture of Canaan,* imagines that her out-of-wedlock child is the offspring of Christ because Jesus had been present during the sexual act that had produced him, or that New Orleans author Valerie Martin writes about in *A Recent Martyr* when she shows the physical and religious pleasure that the young Catholic novitiate Claire receives after strapping herself with a cat o' nine tails. These examples exist within liminal spaces wherein the merging of the sexual and sacred and the real and imagined create new meanings that destabilize the very binaries that help establish them. They exist within real spaces (the church, the bedroom, etc.), but these spaces are imbued with cultural meaning and, because they are racialized or gendered or sexualized or sanctified or regionalized spaces, they exist on both a real and an imagined level.

These spaces are what Homi Bhabha calls, in his introduction to *The Location of Culture*, the "'in-between' spaces" that "provide the terrain for elaborating strategies of selfhood—singular or communal—that initiate new signs of identity, and innovative sites of collaboration, and contestation, in the act of defining the idea of society itself" (2). While Bhabha is concerned primarily with the creation of group or communal identity, his understanding of "sites of collaboration, and contestation" as places where identity is formed lies at the very core of this text and informs all of its analyses as it shows how, in these sites, gendered meaning and identity are created. Judith Butler's *Gender Trouble*, in which she argues that all forms of gender and sexual identity are created as opposed to essential, and are "regulatory fictions," provides important groundwork for the destabilizing of gender identities that may include such elements as race and religion and thus helps fuel definitions of identity in this text. By considering gender a cultural creation, we are able to look at those liminal spaces to see how subjects react when their culturally informed ideas (and ideals) about gender come into conflict or collusion with one another to create "strategies of selfhood" and identity creation.

Bhabha's later observation regarding the work of artist Renee Green is also applicable. In describing her use of stairwells as liminal spaces through which movement is possible, Bhabha writes: "the temporal movement and passage that it [the stairwell] allows, prevents identities at either end of it from settling into primordial polarities. This interstitial passage between fixed identifications opens up the possibility of a cultural hybridity that entertains difference without an assumed or imposed hierarchy" (5). If we view sacred space as one end of the hallway or stairwell and sexual space at the other, then the moments this book examines are the liminal, connective places that exist in between the two, and the subjects who experience them are both progenitors and reflections of the fluid identities and meanings that result. In the case of Rosemary Daniell in the above example, if the stained-glass Jesus exists in the sanctified space of the church, and her boyfriend Troy is present in the youthfully eroticized space of the roller rink, then the imaginative merging of the two images into one, while not occurring in any real sense, creates its own liminal space somewhere between the rink and the church where both may exist without either taking precedence.

But what are the repercussions of the creation of such a space for

Daniell and others who, like her, struggle literarily and personally with the separation of one polarity from another? In the case of southern women, it becomes imperative to examine their cultural surroundings and upbringings to show not only where these separations occur, but what happens when those separations are not maintained. In Reynolds's Oprah-book-club-winning *Rapture of Canaan,* Ninah is faced with just such a dilemma. She tells her sheltered Holiness community that Jesus is the father of her child, but does not deny that she had sex with the child's real father. Instead, she insists that Jesus was the third party in their lovemaking; he was *physically* there, even if he was invisible. The community, of course, cannot accept such a blatantly eroticized Christ, and even when the child is born with his hands fused together, and they take it as a sign from God that he *is* the child of Christ, they refuse to accept that Christ could be linked with sex. Instead, they see the child as a divine gift, tacitly ignoring the sexual act of procreation that gave them the gift. The sacred and the sexual, for the members of Ninah's community, are kept safely at opposite ends of a carefully constructed binary.

The sacred/sexual binary is formed for many authors by and in response to that always amorphous concept—the community. Although the concept of community has (rightfully) come under fire, it has become common in today's southern studies to discuss "The South" and its various inhabitants in terms of imagined communities and shared identifications. There are, as Scott Romine tells us, ways to redefine community that help disentangle the very idea of it from the hegemonic, monolithic, iconic thing it has become. For Romine, community is "enabled by practices of avoidance, deferral, and evasion" and relies "not on what is there so much as what is, by tacit agreement, not there." It is, finally, "a social group that, lacking a commonly held view of reality, coheres by means of norms, codes, and manners that produce a simulated, or at least symbolically constituted, social reality" (3). Some of those gendered and regionalized "norms, codes, and manners" create the "social reality" against which its subjects struggle and through which they eventually find and create what Bhabha calls the "strategies of selfhood," particularly those strategies that allow subjects to make sense of multiple, contested meanings or to attempt to transcend culturally enforced homogenous identities.

One of the first matters that calls for close examination is the concept of the "southern woman." It is a concept with which all of the subjects of this study (both real and imagined) must come to terms. But if we begin with the problem of the southern woman, then we really begin at the problem of the Real. The southern woman, or the "Southern Lady," has been discussed, deconstructed, reconstructed, embraced, and even dismissed entirely by writers, critics, and historians alike. And yet she still persists. *Gone With the Wind* remains a popular purchase or movie rental, and Scarlett O'Hara remains the quintessential southern belle. No matter how strongly southern critics insist that the Southern Lady does not exist, the popularity of such created southern women as the ladies from *Steel Magnolias*, Idgie Threadgoode and Ruthie Jamison from the Whistle Stop Café, or even the elderly Miss Daisy keeps the image of white-skinned, hard-as-nails, soft-as-butter, upper- or upper-middle-class "lady" alive and well. And as long as tourists get off of busses in Atlanta and ask where Rhett and Scarlett are buried, it is an image with which the American South has to contend.[2]

The persistence of such an image in the American cultural mind indicates the strength of desire that Americans have for such a person to be real. In fact, the Southern Lady is one of the most resilient images of personality in American cultural history, and certainly the most resilient where women are concerned. This image, though, with its picture of debutantes and spinsters, its scent of magnolias and lavender, is (of course) the image of someone who does not exist (and never has) as we imagine her. She is an example of Jean Baudrillard's simulacra—a hyperreal person more real to us than reality. But of course she is part of a larger simulacra that is the South itself. A belief in the South, a hegemonic hyperreal nexus of "southern religion," "southern politics," "southern tradition," and so forth, provides much of the training and setting for authors and characters. So, although women in the South spring from different socioeconomic backgrounds, they must all necessarily struggle with these concepts and their ramifications, even when the beliefs and images (e.g., "the southern belle") do not and cannot fit with reality. It is in this liminal space between the real and the hyperreal that such fictional characters exist, and in that space where the most interesting and most troubling incidents occur—the "collisions and collaborations" of identity making.

Perhaps it is this truth that has driven so many southern critics to attempt to define the racialized and gendered realities of women in the South. The hyperreal concepts of the South and its people and the frameworks for them, the traditions, histories, and backgrounds that have created them, and against and amidst which they exist, have been the focus of studies by a burgeoning number of critics in the last three decades. In particular, numerous works have studied southern women's histories, the history of gender and race in the South, and the history and expression of religion by various groups of women in the South. These texts give a clearer, though certainly still muddy, glimpse of the forces that have historically and traditionally made up the southern systems at work in the texts under examination. It will thus be useful to examine some of these texts for the codes and norms that these particular subjects have in common and with which they must contend.

Why not include works by women of color who are in and influenced by the South? While the traditional "southern lady" is almost always white in the mind of Americans, it would be naïve to say that southern culture, including its religious nature, does not have an impact on southern black identity formation. Works by Alice Walker, Gayl Jones, and Octavia Butler, for example, all examine the construction of southern black womanhood in light of the South's racial politics and history. In the end, however, texts such as Butler's *Kindred,* Jones's *Corregidora* and Walker's *Meridian* all examine the formation of black female identity, including sexuality, primarily in terms of the racial politics of the South and slavery rather than in response to particular lessons taught them regarding sexuality, culture or religion, and I chose to narrow my scope to those authors who specifically write about the sexual and spiritual lessons which helped form white female identity.

That identity, however, must be understood in terms of the South's understanding of race as well as its beliefs regarding sexuality and religion. Work by Anne Goodwyn Jones (*Tomorrow Is Another Day: The Woman Writer in the South, 1859–1936*) and Deborah Gray White (*Ar'n't I a Woman? Female Slaves in the Plantation South*) paint a picture of an antebellum South in which the fiction of white southern women as the models of piety, virtue, chastity, and charity is built upon the truth of the violence done against black women in the South. Racist definitions of white womanhood further endangered the lives of black men by constructing them as dangers to a white woman's purity and set black women in direct opposition to white women. And while both black and white women could be said to have suffered at the hands of religious patriarchy in the South, it would be too simplistic to say their suffering resulted from the same sources. As feminist theologian Kwok Pui-Lan writes, "white women's critique of patriarchy is less valid as a tool to analyse black women's oppression because, although white women are oppressed by patriarchy, they at the same time enjoy the protection and privileges accorded to them by the white patriarchal American institutions" (29). It is traditional southern culture's insistence on such protections for the white woman that makes the South a particularly apt example of Pui-Lin's theory.

Writing about the early twentieth-century South, author Lillian Smith makes clear that the separation of the races and the privileging of whiteness was, in fact, foundational to other cultural lessons regarding sex, religion, and the taboos associated with each. She explains that she and other southern girls of her generation were taught by their mothers that the whiteness of their skin went hand-in-hand with virtue, and that forgetting one's race was tantamount to forgetting one's virtue. In particular, intermingling with African Americans, even in play, was akin to engaging in masturbation or sex—two of the biggest prohibitions for "good" girls. She explicitly draws the connection between sexual and racial taboos by using the same language for each: "parts of your body are segregated areas which you must stay away from and keep others away from. These areas you touch only when necessary. In other words, you cannot associate freely with them any more than you can associate freely with colored children" (87). The conflation of lessons regarding sex with those regarding race ensures that such lessons remain interconnected, even if such connections are ultimately unacknowledged or ignored, and so while focusing on the long-term results of southern sexual and religious training, one must keep racial differences in mind, knowing full well the racial nature of southern female identity construction.

Another theoretical issue of concern for southern authors dealing with southern female identity is that of desire and the body, and here too Lillian Smith offers insight into the lessons taught to white southern girls in the first half of the twentieth century. Smith explains that white southern mothers of the middle and upper classes taught that the body was a "Thing of Shame" that "must never be desecrated by pleasures— except for the few properly introduced . . . through pain, however repulsive," which one "must accept as having a right to enter this temple as one accepts visits from disagreeable relatives" (87). In Smith's work, and in later works, we see characters focus on pain in order to make sex (and sexuality) acceptable. Sex, both during Smith's time and later, has been a thing to be endured or painfully withstood—otherwise it becomes a reason for guilt. Thus, women are often taught to relinquish eroticism and desire even while meeting cultural demands to present eroticizable bodies.[3] This will become particularly relevant in Lee Smith's *Saving Grace*, as Grace's father, a preacher, cheats on Grace's mother with younger and younger women after Grace's mother begins to lose her pretty dancing-girl looks.

Desire, however, is a tricky thing. It cannot simply be done away with. It can, however, be sublimated, reimagined, and transferred, and for southern women, religion makes for an easy transference point. Although it is too simple to say that religious passion is simply a sublimation of sexual passion (or vice-versa), it would also be naïve to say that transformation does not occur at all. Before we can address the specific desires of particular characters, however, we must first address the general problem of desire and the questions it begs: What is it? Where does it come from? And, ultimately, how is it expressed? When discussing a theoretical framework for understanding desire, it is impossible to ignore the writings of Rene Girard, and in particular, his groundbreaking work *Deceit, Desire, & the Novel* which deals explicitly with the very nature of desire. No desire, Girard argues, is ever really spontaneous, no matter what it may feel like to the desirous. Instead, desire is mimetic and mediated through a third party. It places a value on the desired object that is directly proportional to the value placed on that same object by the third party, or the mediator. As the mediator's desire (or what the object imagines the mediator's desire is) grows, so too does the object's. While it complicates matters when the mediator is a cultural belief or understanding, the situation becomes even more complex when either the object or the mediator is associated with religion, or the divine. As a less theoretical example, I offer this anecdote from a wedding performed in September 2003 by Southern Baptist preacher Kevin Day. At this wedding, Preacher Day gave a sermon in which he used the symbol of a triangle to represent desire and the relationship between the newly married couple and Jesus. When they begin their relationship, man and woman are at the base of a triangle, and Christ is the apex. As they grow in love for one another, the preacher promised, they would move further up the edges of the triangle, growing not only close to one another, but closer to Jesus as well.

Facing such obvious symbolism as the triangle, one is immediately reminded of Girard's theory of triangulated, or mediated desire, but there are questions to be asked. After all, does this triangulated relationship make Jesus the object? Or does it make the other individual in the relationship the object? The answer is not clear-cut, and the positions of power within the relationship are fluid. If, on the one hand, Jesus is seen as the object of desire, and the human partner is the mediator through which one can identify and know Jesus, then is Jesus and, by default, the divine, made subordinate to the act of desire created by the mortal parties in the relationship? It is not only the questions that are troubling, however. Because Girard argues that the fascination that is engendered in the subject by the mediator often becomes a fascination with the mediator himself, it seems that the mediator acquires, in the mind of the subject, the same characteristics as the originally admired object. When Rosemary Daniell imagines herself "safe, warm, in a blond savior's arms," for example, it is clear that Jesus has taken on the qualities of her young, blond boyfriend. Such merging happens over and again when southern women's fascinations with men are mediated by the divine (and vice-versa).

Girard's theory complicates matters even further when we look at his breakdown of mediated desire into the categories of external and internal. An external mediated desire is one for which the mediator is somehow above and unreachable by the subject, such as, in the wedding example, Jesus. In this case, the newlyweds desire one another through Christ the mediator who is above each of them, but through whom each may increase their desire and love for one another. An internal mediated desire, on the other hand, is a desire for which the mediator and the subject are on the same level and may even interact. To return to the triangle, Christ would then be the object while each newlywed would remain the mediator for the other. If we were to replace Jesus with an extramarital interest, these are the types of desire, as Girard's text examines, that will ultimately lead to jealousy, envy, and even violence.[4] Finally, the results of such triangulation and mediated desire depend largely, of course, on the cultural framework in which the relevant subjects exist, and in the case of works by and about twentieth-century white southern females, that cultural framework is both regional and gendered.

Triangulated desire that has, as its points, two mortals and a representative of the divine, demands definitions of religious and mortal love, or *agape* and *Eros*. While the definitions of these terms have always been hotly debated, the meanings presented in Anders Nygren's classic theological study "Agape and Eros" prove close to those presented throughout the texts of this study and match the definitions of desire given by Girard. His definition of Eros, for example, posits that it is "acquisitive . . . and longing. [It] *recognizes value* in its object and loves it. . . . Eros is determined by the quality, the beauty and worth of its object; it is not spontaneous, but 'evoked,' 'motivated'" (94). Eros can be felt by an individual for another individual *or* for the divine, and it can be sexual or mystical in nature, but it cannot be unmediated. While Eros may recognize value, the object's value is created elsewhere, based on the mediator's assignment of value. Eros is ultimately, according to Nygren, never the result of more than the beholder's view of the value of the object. Agape, on the other hand, is ascribed *to* the divine—it is unmediated and spontaneous. It ascribes value to the desired object instead of the desiring subject because of a priori value.

Where Nygren seems unrealistic, however, is in his stance that humans must attempt to put aside Eros and embrace agape as the only correct form of desire. Instead, agape represents an impossible form of desire for human beings who exist in a world where nothing is unmediated and where desire, even religious desire, is constructed. And thus focus should be placed on Eros as the only form of desire in which changes are even possible. In part, Eros must take precedence as a realistic form of desire because agape ignores the very real physical presence of the body, and it is through the body that much of desire is filtered. Ultimately, as theologian Paul Tillich argues in his famous examination *Dynamics of Faith*, Eros and agape cannot be severed from one another or even viewed separately. It seems, instead, that Eros should encompass *all* forms of yearning desires, be they for divine attachment or mortal pleasures.

Sexual Eros, the form in which Eros is most commonly considered, is a desire for something sexual that the subject takes as an object. Spiritual or mystical Eros, on the other hand, is a desire someone has for whatever he or she perceives to be the divine. Nygren further clarifies that "the most obvious thing about eros is that it is a desire, a longing, a striving," but it can also serve as "the mediator between Divine and human life" (90). Eros itself thus becomes the triangulating force between the individual and his or her divinity. Furthermore, no matter what type of Eros it is, Eros is "patterned on human love" (94) and is unlike agape which is · patterned on God's love for humankind, is unselfish, and ascribes value to its object. The authors chosen for this study do not deal with agape; instead, they combine the two forms of Eros, so that they (and their characters) may ultimately move back and forth between eroticizing Christ and exalting mortal partners, sometimes simultaneously. Although the characters do not often consciously recognize this mingling of Eros, the authors of their texts use conscious manipulations and juxtapositions of Christ and Christian imagery with erotic imagery and thought throughout their works to show how the two become ultimately inseparable, especially for southern females.

These late twentieth-century works—novels, short stories, poems and autobiographies from Lee Smith, Rosemary Daniell, Sheri Reynolds, Connie May Fowler, Dorothy Allison, and Valerie Martin—all examine these inseparable forms of Eros. However, it would be naïve to ignore the roles that earlier southern female authors such as Augusta Jane Evans, Kate Chopin, and Flannery O'Connor have played in showing how deeply damaging is the attempt to distance spiritual Eros from other forms of Eros (in particular, as here, sexual Eros). Evans's 1896 best-selling *St. Elmo* represents a precursor to such twentieth-century literature, offering a heroine, Edna Earl, whose attraction to and desire for the rakish St. Elmo must be put on hold as she dedicates her life to religious service. She can eventually marry him only when he himself becomes a minister and representative of God-on-earth, worthy of her submission. Twentieth-century author Rosemary Daniell will later write that such a "god man" was, for her, a "necessary male link in [the] future ascent to the arms of Jesus" (*Fatal Flowers* 39). Chopin, whose subtle stories often escaped the understanding of her contemporary readers, also explores the connection between the spiritual and the physical in her story "Two Portraits (The Nun and the Wanton)." In the story, the young girl Alberta is sketched twice—in the first sketch, she grows to become a prostitute, reveling in and unable to see anything but her sensuality. In a second sketch, she becomes a nun, cloistered away from the sensual world and experiencing ecstatic religious visions. Neither outcome is particularly wholesome, and neither extreme (one, the spirit without the flesh, and the other, the flesh without the spirit) seems overly promising. The wanton is entirely dependent upon a fleeting beauty to sustain existence, and the nun, as pointed out by Emily Smith-Riser, "is fulfilled to a ridiculously ecstatic, orgasmic extreme—and it is not physical, only imaginary" (24).

This attempt to separate flesh and spirit and to deny one aspect of the self in favor of another shows up also in the works of O'Connor. Although her novel *Wise Blood* has been studied extensively, it is worth mentioning Hazel Motes, the self-proclaimed anti-preacher and reluctant mystic of the novel. In his 1988 study of O'Connor's works, *Flannery O'Connor and the Mysteries of Love*, Richard Giannone examines the travels of Hazel Motes through phases of carnality, self-exaltation, and repentance, explaining that Hazel's first "evil" is in "replacing the relationship one should have to God with the relationship one sets up with the body" (18). Through his relationship with Leora Watts, Hazel replaces the spirit with the body, but the second, and more prolonged evil comes about as a result of Hazel's attempt to live solely by his own rules and by denying that he needs to be forgiven. Such an attempt will ultimately lead, as it often does in O'Connor's works, to a painful conversion. Committing murder is, by the rules of Hazel's new self-praising religion, no worse than fornication with Leora Watts, and Hazel eventually has to find the spirit in the same way he has denied it—through the flesh. Burning his eyes out, subjecting himself to poverty, hunger, and further self-mutilation, and exposing himself to the elements are all forms of physical suffering he forces himself to undergo as penance for denying the spiritual in favor of the physical and mental. This penance results finally in peace, but it is a peace that O'Connor insists be painfully wrought out of the flesh.[5]

Although all of these authors—both the earlier ones and the late twentieth-century ones—come from different backgrounds and the specific works in question span a number of decades, the thematic energy of these texts is clearly focused towards a similar goal, that of finding a way to internalize and combine spiritual and sexual growth. Ultimately, however, it is the authors who came after O'Connor who have been able to more overtly discuss issues such as physical suffering, bodily desires, and spiritual hungers. The Women's Rights movement and, later, second-wave feminism would give women authors the courage, leeway, and power to write more openly about their lives and their bodies. Rosemary Daniell, whose early poetry absolutely reflects a kind of "angry feminism" that existed in the 1970s, provides one of our first examples of the post-O'Connor southern woman writer dealing with religion. While Daniell's spiritual views ultimately differ from O'Connor's, her influences are similar, and her concerns are often the same. Not only Daniell but other women authors benefited from the anger of those early feminists, and their works are instrumental in understanding the sexual and sacred ideals of femininity in the South, and what happens when such ideals come into contact, conflict, and collusion.

Before we can examine the texts, however, we must engage in what is, by all accounts, an impossible task—formulating or at least contextualizing an identity for the white, southern woman in the twentieth century. John Lynxwiler and Michele Wilson, in "The Code of the New Southern Belle," remind us that such a woman is an amalgam of images created through historical, literary, and sociological sources; she is everything from a "down home" church mother to a trash-talking "Sweet Potato Queen."[6] In order, however, to understand the religious and sexual couplings that occur in the writing of so many southern female writers, a brief look at the literary history of southern women and their historical, religious, and sexual surroundings will be useful. Such an examination should illuminate the transition from antebellum southern female identity to contemporary images of the "new" southern woman.

Such contextualizing of the southern woman should begin with a brief overview of Christianity in the South that, while not intended to be a detailed examination of southern religion, helps to make clear the historical and cultural contexts for the accepted and encouraged roles of white, southern females. There are a number of studies currently in publication on southern religion, but Samuel Hill, Randall Miller and Charles Regan Wilson are, without doubt, three of the best known and prolific authors on the topic, and most of the information drawn together here comes from their work. One thing that all three have in common is the understanding that southerners (and their religion) are different from northerners and the rest of the world primarily because *they* see themselves as different. Whatever else we may have to say about identity formation, it is impossible to deny that identity, particularly group identity, is often formed in relation to and in opposition against an outside entity. This holds particularly true for religious identity formation in the South prior to the Civil War.

Before the war, southern Christians of many denominations differed from their northern counterparts in their attempts to use religion to support the system of slavery, and, in the 1840s, in moves that have yet to be undone, the three major denominations of Christianity in the South all broke from their mother churches primarily over this issue. The Baptists formed the Southern Baptist Convention, while the Methodists founded the Methodist Episcopal Church, South, and the Presbyterians (having already separated once into "Old School" and "New School" Presbyterians) created The Presbyterian Church in the Confederate States of America, all three groups insisting that they were more adequately prepared to deal with the southerner's particular religious needs. That sense of separate identity was only exacerbated by the loss of the war. Wilson points out that the religious separation of the South from the North "was more enduring than the political separation. After the Civil War ended, none of the three religious families reunited, so that the southern churches became the repositories of the southern identity, the prime institutional embodiment of southern regionalism, and the treasuries of the region's religious folklife" (*Judgment* 5). In essence, the very identity of the South became a religious one wherein the differences between the various Protestant denominations were less than the differences between the northern and southern branches of those denominations.

Although obviously neither as popular nor as large as the Protestant denominations, the Catholic Church also had a significant presence in the South both before and after the Civil War. In New Orleans, of course, the Catholic Church found a strong foothold, but even in the rural areas of Mississippi, Tennessee, and Alabama, there were congregations of Catholics tucked in amongst the Baptists and Methodists. These churches survived not by being different or serving the needs only of their followers, but by opening their doors and serving the community at large. On "the frontier, especially," Randall Miller tells us, "Southerners took what religion came their way. Baptists, Presbyterians, Catholics, whatever, all gathered to hear an itinerant preacher," and "such common experiences blurred theology and polity enough to fuse the assembled worshipers into a Christian fellowship—at least for the moment" (8). Even once Catholic communities began to grow in the South, however, those communities were different from the ones in the North in ways that made them more acceptable to southern Protestants. Southern Catholic communities were smaller and less populated by immigrants than the large parishes in the northern cities, and the impoverished nature of the small parishes lessened a traditional form of hostility that northern Catholics suffered—namely that the Catholic Church was somehow suspiciously well off and thus distanced from the rural "every man."

Ultimately, however, the most significant factor in Catholic acceptance was, without a doubt, the willingness of the Catholic Church to approve the southern status quo, particularly in regard to slavery. Like their Protestant brethren, Catholics in the South were divided from others throughout the country by the issue of slavery, and, as a result, often had more in common with southern Protestants than northern Catholics. Miller sums up the Catholic Church's attitude in the antebellum South when he says that "the Church recognized its minority status in an overwhelmingly Protestant society and assumed a low political and social profile for much of the antebellum period. Church leaders embraced Southern attitudes regarding slavery . . . and reminded detractors of Catholic contributions to American national development" (7).[7] The social acceptance achieved by the Catholic Church, however, did not raise it completely above suspicion. Southerners were wary of the immigrant nature of the larger parishes, such as those located in the upper South and New Orleans, and the adherence of Catholics to the word of a Pope situated in a foreign country caused southerners to question their loyalties. Such concerns and suspicions became less important in the postbellum South, however, when southern Catholics, just like southern Protestants, turned their attention to the loss of the Civil War. Catholic congregations in the late nineteenth century memorialized the Confederate dead and joined the Protestant churches in attempting to rebuild a spiritual South that was forced to find a new identity for itself.

This new postbellum identity of the white South was a complex and sophisticated one for both Protestants and Catholics, and it was based primarily on the loss of the Civil War. Charles Reagan Wilson examines this identity and its formation as a religious one in his important study *Baptized in Blood: The Religion of the Lost Cause, 1865–1920*. In *Baptized*, and later in *Judgment & Grace in Dixie: Southern Faiths from Faulkner to Elvis*, Wilson argues that, while historians and critics may not exactly know when a "southern identity" first emerged, it's clear that "the Civil War experience and Confederate defeat surely gave a new meaning to that identity as a separate southern people within the American nation" (*Judgment* 19). The loss of the Civil War brought southerners together in ways, he maintains, that were similar to the war itself. Instead of seeing themselves joined in a common cause, however, southerners began to see themselves as a "tragic" people specifically chosen by God to suffer. In an eerily prescient moment of Augusta Jane Evans's propagandistic Civil War novel *Macaria*, the self-sacrificing heroine Irene sacrifices her father and her true love to the war, calling upon God to "crown the South" with independence in return for the loss of her loved ones. Her romanticization of and pride in her own suffering for the sake of her homeland foreshadows the loss of the war and this rise of the religion of the Lost Cause. Her appeal to God makes clear the South's understanding of its cause as a religious one—which makes it both more devastating and more important when they lose. Having their pride humbled through defeat, southerners would eventually compensate through the mythification of that defeat. They did not lose because God turned away from the South—instead, they lost because God was paying special attention to them and strengthening them for a spiritual struggle to come. The South would thus learn to see itself no longer as merely a political region, but as a religious one, specially endowed by God to fight for souls.

By focusing on their loss as a religious message, southerners were able to turn attention inward on themselves and their region, separating themselves from northerners and northern religions. A tour of Catholic houses of worship dating back to Reconstruction shows that Catholics, no less so than Protestants, saw a religious message in the loss of the war. Many Catholic churches flew the battle flags of the Lost Cause and had memorial statues dedicated to the Confederate dead. Diana Pasulka tells us that at St. Anne's Church in Sumter, South Carolina, there is even "a rare display of stained-glass windows dedicated to deceased Confederate soldiers, and more generally to the southern defeat" and that these windows, like more traditionally religiously themed ones "are a significant part of how the deceased are made present to South Carolina catholics" (293). By incorporating images of the "Lost Cause" into its space of worship, the Catholic Church places its regional identity on a level with its religious one.

It is unsurprising that regional and religious identity became intertwined after the war. As a chosen people, southerners of all denominations saw themselves, Samuel Hill argues, "as uniquely equipped with the spiritual resources and dedication to wage the war" against "a world prostituting itself" (*Religion and the Solid South,* 375). As Wilson argues, "southerners came to believe that God had not abandoned them but instead had chastised them, in preparation for a greater destiny in the future" (20). The belief in a "greater destiny" allowed the postwar South to see itself as a spiritual stronghold in a world where religious orthodoxy was fading in the light of nineteenth-century social and economic reforms.

An enduring conservative religious orthodoxy is, in fact, a long accepted trait of the "southern identity," and one which helps to explain why, as the century turned and the new millennium began, the white South held on to older ideas not only about what was religiously acceptable, but about what was culturally acceptable as well. In particular, the role of women in the South continued to resonate with an eighteenth- and nineteenth-century "feel" well into the mid-twentieth century, and Anne Firor Scott's work on white antebellum women helps lay the groundwork for studying this transition from the prewar to the postwar South. Throughout the nineteenth century, she explains, southern white women were "preoccupied with personal piety, with the need for salvation and for goodly behavior" in part because "the image of the ideal Christian woman was very close to the image of the ideal southern lady so that religion strongly reinforced the patriarchal culture" (92). Those traits that many attribute to the mythological "southern lady" are strongly influenced by a conservative Christian outlook. One of these traits is that the southern woman must be absolutely concerned with salvation—her own and others'—and she must lead those non-followers that she knows and loves to convert. Fred Hobson has pointed out that the idea of conversion has always been important to the predominant Christian religions in the South; in fact, proof of conversion is so vital that the very structure of conversion narratives has influenced other twentieth-century southern writings such as race narratives,[8] but Scott's argument is that women, more so than men, have always been the ones expected to secure those conversions.

Women, Scott suggests, were seen as having greater power to "bring men, not naturally so inclined, to virtuous habits" (113), and such expectations did not disappear in the twentieth century. In a fairly recent study conducted at a Southern Baptist Church, Carolyn Pevey, Christine Williams, and Christopher Ellison found that "the issue of wifely obedience is sometimes linked with the traditional role of the Christian woman as the bearer of religion within the household: In modern classes and sermons, women are told to make their husbands (better) Christians by manifesting a quiet, gentle spirit" (142). It is however this very expectation that will prove so difficult for many of the subjects of this study. In considering her mother's suicide, for example, Rosemary Daniell realizes that her mother, Melissa Ruth Connell, "was convinced until she died" that "if she had been good enough, . . . [her husband] would have been better" (*Fatal Flowers*, 45), and in Connie May Fowler's *Before Women Had Wings,* Glory Marie can't help but wonder if her husband's abandonment of his family and his eventual suicide are somehow connected to her inability to be a "good" woman for him.

The desire to be "good enough" to keep a family intact and to keep men from "backsliding" is a desire that finds expression in southern women's literature reaching much further back than Fowler and Daniell. In her postbellum novel *St. Elmo,* Augusta Jane Evans turns from proactively pro-Confederate political novels to the sentimental story of a young, religious woman who devotes her life to being a good southern woman. Edna Earl dedicates her life and her work to God, putting God and her love for him above all secular matters, but she finds herself falling in love with the rakish St. Elmo Murray. When it becomes clear to her that she cannot save him, she realizes she must leave him and decides to, instead, write a book that will ultimately save all sinners who read it. Even though she spends the rest of the novel unable to avoid thinking about St. Elmo, she realizes that she can only enter into a relationship with him after he becomes a better Christian, and so she focuses her own life on securing conversions in the thinly veiled hope that his will ultimately be one of them.

In fact, the expectations of "goodness" and the ability to bring people to salvation fall into a subset of expectations of service to others that seem to extend historically over women in the South. Many of the essays in the well-known collection *Southern Women* edited by Caroline Matheny Dillman argue that women of all social classes in the South have been expected to care and take on responsibility for others, whether they were husbands, families, extended families, sick neighbors, or even visiting strangers. William Kenkel and Sarah Shoffner write that "home and family [are] supposed to be central in [the southern woman's] life" and that "personality traits compatible with her life included meekness, self-control, self-abnegation, and long suffering patience" (163). In fact, "long suffering patience" is almost a hallmark of the white southern woman, and those females who have suffered loudly, or who have not exhibited patience, have often been seen or depicted as overly aggressive or even masculine. Even the infamous Scarlett O'Hara, known for her attempts to thwart the southern systems of patriarchy, wants desperately to be like her gentle, uncomplaining mother at first, and continuously feels guilty that she is not more like the quietly religious woman. Such beliefs regarding the "naturally" religious nature of women and the roles that they must play were believed by southerners to have come from the Bible itself. Joanne V. Hawks writes that Christian southerners, whatever their denomination, believed that "the Bible taught that God did not mean for women to assume . . . public responsibilities" (81), but only those responsibilities of caring for the home and the people who resided and visited therein.

While Scott and others discuss the ways in which southern women were responsible for religious upbringing in the antebellum South, anthropologist Valerie Fennell considers why these religious duties were initially turned over to women. She cites the work of Barbara Welter, who explains that "U.S. men in the nineteenth century became materialists working such long hours that they could not keep the religious traditions of their forebears for want of time to do so. Instead, they turned these duties over to their wives or other women in their families" (140).

Certainly lack of time may have been one of the original reasons why men ceded religious duties to women. However, a number of other factors, such as southern propaganda regarding the "natural" godly, virtuous, and conversional abilities of women and their socially dictated roles in rearing children, most certainly lent themselves to the continuance of this tradition. Furthermore, as Fennell herself points out, the men never actually gave over positions of power within the church to women. While women were expected to serve the church and further conversions within society, they were not leaders: "only men were ministers, and it was always preferable even in voluntary church work to have a man in a leadership position over any group of women. . . . Masculinity was associated with leadership, and the higher the rank the more likely men were to assume the position" (143). Even within the Pentecostal religion, one that is "egalitarian in its belief that all 'saints' both male and female, have the right and even the obligation to openly express their joyful worship of God," there is still a prohibition on women—"women can be preachers, yes, but at the same time they must be careful not to emulate men or threaten male authority" (110). Despite the liberating potentials of a "woman's place" in religion, the actual roles afforded women were still situated within the strongly hierarchal strata of religion and southern culture.

Once established, the religious duties allowed to and expected of women essentially served to lock them into a number of restricted roles. Critic Jean Friedman writes that "the rural kin-oriented, church-related society limited the evolution of a southern women's culture" (6). Even though a woman's church culture may have existed, it was one that was more limiting than expanding. In fact, the patriarchal, religious, family-oriented networks that permeated lower, middle- and upper-middle-class white southern society during the mid-twentieth century further limited the growth of women's roles in society because "male control of evangelical family churches insured a double standard of church discipline which reinforced traditional sexual roles and deterred formation of independent women's organizations" (8). Further, starting early in southern Christian communities, women were shunned and punished for their digressions whereas men were not,[9] and male heads of the church and family effectively worked together to keep the status quo.

That this "traditional" southern religious culture is a patriarchal one is obvious, but less clear is that it was, and often still is, the paradoxical role of southern women to not only maintain their own submissiveness, but to pass it on to their daughters. This contradictory expectation is perhaps what Shirley Abbot refers to when she writes: "to grow up female in the South is to inherit a set of directives that warp one for life. . . . [T]he legacy passed from mother to daughter is everywhere ambivalent and complex, full of unconfessed wishes and unadmitted bequests, woven with demands and admonitions, some of which contradict the rest" (148). This "legacy" continued to be passed down by southern women well into the twentieth century, and it is one that called for submissiveness to men and compliance with traditional gender roles. Valerie Fennel writes even more explicitly that, even now, "Everybody gets, and passes on, the patriarchal message. . . . [T]o make another generation of the family and to please Momma and Daddy, girls have to agree to the rules of female subservience," and "the families of little girls mirror and reinforce the societal devaluation of women and thus offer no refuge or protection from it" (140–41).

In 1972, the Southern Baptist Convention codified these "rules of female subservience" and went so far as to adopt a resolution that cited Eve's role in Adam's fall from Eden and reaffirmed "God's order of authority for his church and his Christian home: 1) Christ the head of every man; 2) man the head of every woman" (124). This resolution was reaffirmed in the 1980s, and in 1981, the SBC also reiterated that it absolutely does not "endorse the Equal Rights Amendment."[10] Finally, Caroline Matheny Dillman proposes that "Southern women are tied to men for validation" and that southern women "seemed to want to maintain the ideal for their daughters" (16). The roles and legacies of antebellum *and* twentieth-century women explored by Fennell, Scott, and others support Dillman's conclusion that "it seems to be extremely difficult for contemporary southern women to let go of almost two hundred years of socialization that has impressed upon them the importance of family and of adherence to the prescriptions of what a good southern woman should be" (16).

But if southern women were and are supposed to be saviors and servers, they have been up against some fierce opposition. Where women have been taught they must be saintly, men were expected to be the exact opposite. As Fennell explains, the "good ol' boys" of southern society were and are taught that "excessive drinking, sexual escapades with women, . . . brawling and fighting with other men and gambling" are proper and accepted behavioral outlets (141). Southern historian Ted Ownby similarly writes that "[t]he aggressiveness and toughness of male culture clashed with the softness and humility" of religion (134). His study *Subduing Satan* posits that "white southern culture in the late nineteenth century displayed a profound tension between a hell-raising aggressiveness located wherever men gathered away from home and an evangelical culture centered in the home and church that stressed harmony, self-control, and the special religious virtues of women" (372). These assumed virtues of course lead to what he calls a very "shaky tension" by the twentieth century because, while women have been expected to "save" or convert their husbands, men have traditionally been expected to resist the teaching of Christianity.

Critic Margaret Wolfe gives an example of the type of complicated relationship that can result from differing gender expectations. She tells the story of a southern man who, after attending church with his girlfriend one night, questioned her about her commitment to religion. When she explained that she was very religious, he doubted her, telling her that she "did not have no more religion than [his] ass," and then he "screwed her before he got home" to prove it (116). The implications here are not only that men are more disdainful of religion, but also that religion and sex are incompatible. If the sexually active woman in the anecdote does not have "religion," then it apparently falls upon her male partner to prove such a thing and thus shoulder no share of the blame. In fact, for decades, women were considered at fault if their men became overly aroused, and women were even warned that letting their partners go "too far" could result in illness or death. Karen, the young female protagonist in Lee Smith's "Tongues of Fire" is even told by her mother that "petting . . . is cruel to the boy . . . because he has no control over himself. . . . It is all up to the girl . . . and if he cannot find relief, then the poison will all back up into his organs, causing pain and sometimes death" (115). While such an argument strikes twenty-first-century readers as patriarchal propaganda, such teachings were (and still are in some cases) handed down as truth in order to help keep southern females away from activities that might lead to sex.

If, as Fennell explains, "these behaviors that men consider vital for

the demonstration of their masculinity are usually discouraged in religious settings" (141), then the romantic/sexual pairings of southern men
and women had and have the potential to be devastating as they set up
impossibly competing gender goals. Women, in particular, are supposed
to be both chaste and sexual while appealing to men's secular natures
in an attempt to make them religious. The resulting conundrum often
leads to confusion about the very nature of sexuality and its acceptable outlets. Sexuality, in fact, has long been another source of guilt for
southern women as they mature. As clarified by critics John Lynxwiler
and Michele Wilson, southern girls in the mid-twentieth century, those
referred to by the authors as "New Southern Belles," must "emphasize
chaste sexuality," while at the same time existing as sexualized orna-
ments for men: "Rather than opting for achievement on her own, [the
New Southern Belle] achieves through affiliations with men. The ability
to achieve is dependent on being male oriented. . . . Since she assumes
that males operate on the basis of their hormones, she dresses to please
him and sharpens to a razor's edge her skills in coquetry. Sexuality based
on traditional sex role distinctions is paramount" (117). Women thus
have dual roles—they must be chaste, pristine, and celibate, but they
must also be sexual and alluring to men.

In considering the southern white woman and those influences upon
her identity, we must finally return to the propensity of the postbellum
South to romanticize loss and suffering. While it is certainly true that
suffering has long been considered an appropriate emotion for religious
women,[11] the South managed to take the idea of loss to a new and romantic height after the end of the Civil War in the form of the "Lost
Cause." Because postbellum southerners saw themselves as separate
from northerners and chosen by God for great suffering, the very act
of suffering became a regional issue. Wilson's arguments that southerners felt that the South "represented the last stronghold of pure religion"
(29), and that "they had been destined to crusade with honor for a cause
they saw as right, but they had been destined to lose and suffer" (21)
forges a link between the act of religious suffering and the identity of the
South. Women in the South, who were further taught by prevailing religious beliefs that they must suffer for men, who were natural extensions
of Christ and God, developed a particularly strong romantic attachment
to the act of suffering.

Sociologist Sam Hill writes about a woman "who could hardly bear the sound of her husband tuning his violin" and yet said nothing, "dedicated as she was to the ideal of self-sacrifice" (*Solid South* 99). Women were made to "suffer and to be strong" (99) because they owed it to men to suffer out of gratitude for economic caretaking and to God out of desire for salvation. Hill explains that, for antebellum southern women, the most important aspects of religious life included "the needs for constant cultivation of submissiveness to the will of an all powerful God," "the achievement of conversion and secure salvation," and "a strong sense of one's own innate wickedness" (95). For the white southern woman in the post–Civil War South, who, like other southerners, had internalized the belief that "God had not abandoned them but instead had chastised them, in preparation for a greater destiny in the future" (Wilson, *Judgment* 20), sacrifice and its outward manifestation, suffering, was thus proof that they were not only aware of their own "innate wickedness," but had found a way to transcend it.

Christian religious doctrine of the nineteenth century further taught that women must "inhabit the sphere to which God had appointed them" and that "all sin consists in selfishness and all holiness or virtue in disinterested benevolence" (Hill, *Solid South* 94). Although such ideas were also part of the larger movement towards the "cult of true womanhood," they had a particularly strong "staying power" in the South, and southern women, who were so well indoctrinated to the ideas of sacrifice and suffering, not only tended to forego their own desires, but also instilled such values in their female children. Expectations were passed down through the nineteenth and well into the twentieth centuries, and are continuously propagated not only by male-headed churches and organizations in the South, but also by mothers and grandmothers, the very victims of such a system. It is thus no wonder that, within the religious South, women and girls gathered to them—like flies to honey—guilt, anxiety, depression, and inexplicable hungers and cravings. And it is ultimately this complex nexus of feelings and forbidden desires that lead to emotional sublimations, substitutions, and mergings.

This nexus, a theoretical space created out of a cultural context, finds a home in both physical and imagined spaces and the elements associated with those spaces. In particular, the cultural artifacts associated with religion—hymns, prayers, and religious iconography (or even lack thereof)—combine to create, particularly in Southern Baptist and evangelical churches and especially for female children and teenagers, an early sexualized space where teaching regarding bodily taboos and religion leads to erotic fantasies of Christ as a first boyfriend or sexual partner. Michel Foucault's theories regarding heterotopic spaces help to reveal the places where fantasies are either set free or restrictively controlled in forming sexual identity. For example, early lessons about what are and are not acceptable outlets for physical desires for females lead girls away from openly exploring physical sexuality, but because no one can simply "escape" physical sexuality, girls will often sublimate their early desires and confusions into the "appropriate" religious venues (church choirs, helping the poor, Sunday school, revivals, etc.) This act of sublimation creates what Foucault calls a heterotopia—a space where the two desires, religious and secular, combine. These spaces can be (and often are) churches themselves (the literal site of the taboo), or they can be the usual spaces for erotic fantasies—the bedroom, bathroom, closet, or other favorite hideaways such as hidden clearings in the forest, caves, or even, in the case of one author, an abandoned dumping ground. For Daniell, Smith, and Reynolds in particular, these spaces encompass almost all of the above.

In the works of Fowler, Daniell, and Smith, the heterotopic moment becomes more complicated as female characters find in their lovers replacements for parents, both mortal and divine. Fowler's character Avocet (Bird for short), in *Before Women Had Wings,* makes explicit the connection between her mother and a capricious Old Testament God while imagining for herself a romantic relationship with God's son, Jesus. In her novel *The Problem with Murmur Lee,* Fowler draws the connection between parents and the divine and, ultimately, sexuality, when she shows how a young girl with epilepsy reimagines her disease as religious ecstasy in order to draw the attention of her distant, religious mother, only to eventually find a replacement for both her parents and her early religious desires in passionate sex. Smith's Florida Grace Shepherd in *Saving Grace* also draws comparisons, both consciously and unconsciously, between her father and the divine. Her father resembles Jesus in ways both physical and emotional, and Grace's first erotic attraction is to her half-brother, a dead-ringer for her preacher father physically and in matters secular and spiritual. Every lover she takes seems to reflect her early fascination with her father and his overt sexuality. Daniell also does battle in her autobiographical and poetic writings with the desire to seek out "Jesus men," and to fulfill her earliest sexual fantasies of Jesus as the perfect romantic partner. In later sexual relationships with women, she seeks missing parental connections, creating in her desires for women a desire for a feminized, motherly Jesus who bleeds and suffers as women do. The work of Caroline Bynum Walker helps provide a framework for looking at Jesus as both woman and parent. And by examining what may seem to be (and often are) incestuous desires in characters from these southern authors, readers can see the complexities that are created when young southern women conflate images of parents with images of the divine, especially considering the creation of the "sacred erotic."

In some of the most recent texts, those by Dorothy Allison, Valerie Martin, and Sheri Reynolds, we see authors who have found, either through their own lives or through the lives of their characters, value in the act of suffering, both sexually and religiously, and who thus create new spaces in which to examine the nexus of sexuality and faith. Drawing upon studies of traditional Christian mystics and their experiences with pain and religious ecstasy, I examine modern mystical practices in the texts of these authors, uncovering deeper meanings of suffering and masochism than are traditionally granted them. For example, Ninah Huff, the fourteen-year-old protagonist of Reynolds's *Rapture of Canaan*, convinced that her unborn child is the result of sex she had with both her boyfriend *and* Christ, uses physical pain to relate to Jesus and find a path to religious fulfillment. While she will eventually give up the suffering, it is only because of the act of suffering itself that she can move forward. Valerie Martin's characters, on the other hand, find fulfillment through a continuing cycle of what might be termed physical masochism. But unlike the often discussed desire of a masochist to destroy her own sense of self, Martin's characters seek an ultimate *union* of the self with an other—either with a mortal partner or a divine one—that will nullify the emptiness that seems to encompass southern white women who are taught that the sacrifice of the self for a male partner is the ultimate feminine duty. Such works as Martin's, Allison's and Reynolds's question the very definitions of sadomasochism and how it fits into both secular and religious ecstasy.

The practices of contemporary southern Christian culture reflect the literary and theoretical work of southern authors and historians. By looking at the ways in which real spaces such as mega-churches and imagined spaces such as those on the Internet have changed the shape and landscape of Christian religion for women, readers can see how Foucault's and Bhabha's works on heterotopic and interstitial spaces are reflected in real-world examples. Ultimately, the popularity of cultural moments such as purity balls, chastity promises, Christian websites, online ministries, and even "re-virgination" beliefs keep the spaces of sexuality and the sacred at the very forefront of contemporary studies of both.

CHAPTER 2

Erotic Churches and Sacred Bedrooms

The present epoch will perhaps be above all the epoch of space. We are in the epoch of simultaneity: we are in the epoch of juxtaposition, the epoch of the near and far, of the side-by-side, of the dispersed.
—MICHEL FOUCAULT, "Of Other Spaces"

Space, in contemporary discourse . . . has taken on an almost palpable existence, its contours, boundaries, and geographies are called upon to stand in for all the contested realms of identity.
—ANTHONY VIDLER, *The Architectural Uncanny*

In his posthumously released essay "Of Other Spaces," Michel Foucault defines what he calls a heterotopia, or a heterotopic space as a real or socially constructed space in which multiple, often opposing and incompatible meanings can exist at once. These heterotopias, however, can be more than just places where these opposite meanings exist; they can be places that are actually constructed through the interaction and/or collision of those opposing ideas, the places where Homi Bhabha says identities are often formed. Utopias, Foucault argues, are "sites with no real place. . . . [T]hey present society itself in a perfected form, or else society turned upside down" (24). Much work has been done on the construction and destruction of utopias and dystopias, but heterotopias, he says, are "something like counter-sites, a kind of effectively enacted utopia in which the real sites, all the other sites that can be found within the culture, are simultaneously represented, contested, and inverted" and are "outside of all places, even though it may be possible to indicate their location in reality" (24). The experience that lies between the utopia and the heterotopias he calls the mirror. The mirror, he argues, "is a placeless place," and in it the viewer sees "an unreal, virtual space that opens up behind the surface." The mirror "functions as a heterotopia in this respect: it makes this place that I occupy at the moment when I look at myself in the glass at once absolutely real, connected with all the space that surrounds it, and absolutely unreal, since in order to be perceived, it has to pass through this virtual point which is over there" (26). If the mirror functions as a heterotopia, though, it also functions as a site of construction. The existence of the space inside (or behind) the mirror does not exist without a viewer. So the "unreal, virtual space" is one that is, at least partially, constructed by the viewer. Further, when looking in a mirror, the viewer sees herself as interpreted by her own expectations, desires, and fears—and so the virtual viewer in the unreal space is as much constructed as the space she occupies.

Another trait of the heterotopia is that it is often "linked to slices in time" or what Foucault calls "heterochronies" (26). These heterochronies exist where "men arrive at a sort of absolute break with their traditional time." Places such as museums, libraries, or cemeteries exist in real space, but time in these places is at odds with traditional time. Instead, multiple times may be collected through artifacts or even stopped, as in the case of the cemetery. While time around the cemetery and even in the cemetery itself is continuing onward, there is a sense, while in those spaces, that time has ceased—and for the residents of a cemetery, psychic time has indeed come to a close. In the South, it is easy to argue, time has not moved at the same rate as elsewhere in the country. Historian George Rable makes the point that the post–Civil War South even took pride in "being able to quarantine their homes, churches and schools from the forces of modernity that threatened to destroy traditional values" (2–3). That this pride in "tradition" still exists has been made clear by many southern critics and theorists who continue to show the relevancy today of such time-stamped ideas as the Plantation Myth and the Southern Belle. In fact, just as the myth of the glorious southern plantation was created in response to and as a result of feelings of disappointment and failure, the image of the Southern Belle was in many ways a reaction to gender codes of the South that, as modernity progressed, were impossible to follow. Michele Wilson and John

Lynxwiler explain, half tongue-in-cheek that, "as with most stereotypes, true Southern belles were something of a rarity in the Old South; however, they are approaching commonplace in modern times" (114). Like the mirror/heterotopia, the South (or what we imagine as the South in some cases) exists both outside of regular time and as a site of dramatically conflicting and constructed ideas of modernity and tradition.

Because its religious identity has in part caused the South to cling to its beliefs about tradition and value, physical churches themselves are often sites of heterotopic spaces and constructions. Rosemary Daniell is attending a church service when the combined images of her young boyfriend and the stained-glass Jesus give her a "vision of myself raised high, safe, warm in a blond savior's arms" (102). In this moment, the real space of the church becomes one containing both secular and sacred meanings. She is erotically whisked away (at least in her mind) not by her boyfriend, but by a savior. Although he was speaking of Catholic masses in particular, Paul Evdokimov might have been speaking of this scene at Daniell's Baptist service when he compellingly writes that people "are taught by the Liturgy, where ritual, dogma, and art are intimately interwoven. Its images are symbols; our gaze does not stop with them, but uses them as a starting point to ascend to the domain of the invisible" (84). Daniell internalizes these "lessons" regarding the symbolism of religion as she watches Troy pray. Her gaze does not stop with Jesus or with her boyfriend—instead, she creates a new heterotopic space, existing both in and outside of reality (that is, in the "domain of the invisible"). In such a place, liminal as it may be, she is able to enjoy both the eroticism of fantasy and the religious pleasure of being saved without the guilt normally associated with the erotic. The spaces (both real and imagined) thus serve multiple competing functions, as a coping mechanism against guilt and a site for pleasure, and they allow for opposing meanings of eroticism and sacred mysticism.

The reason churches are often the sites of such constructions has to do with what Foucault calls "a certain number of oppositions that remain inviolable." He is uncertain whether such oppositions, such as the one between private and public space, will ever allow society to reach "the point of a practical desanctification of space" (23). Buildings such as churches, however, where people engage in both public and private forms of worshipful behavior, break down the boundaries between private and public, creating a liminal space wherein communal worship exists only in tandem with individual prayer and belief. Churches thus become sites where meaning is created from the collusion of the private and the public, and in the South, as we have seen, the church has traditionally been one of the predominant creators of meaning. It is, after all, through the church that many heteronormative gender ideals are passed down to new generations of southerners—even in the modern age. O. Kendall White Jr. and Daryl White, in their 1995 volume of essays, *Religion in the Contemporary South*, attempt to find exactly the ways in which southern churches continue to do this cultural work of constructing meaning and guiding experience since, in a society increasingly concerned with multiculturalism, pluralism, and cultural relativism, it is hard to see such heterogeneity and tradition as simply a by-product of culture. Instead, Scott Lee Thumma says in his essay in the White and White volume, that "increasingly, to be a southerner will mean to adopt the label and characterization through a process of conscious and intentional choice" (151). It is this choice—to be culturally "southern" or not, that so many of the women in this study struggle with. If, after the Civil War, the South chose to see itself as different, it was a difference only from the rest of the world; it did not embrace difference on an individual level. Pre-constructed identity categories, long in place, continue to exist, and women have had to choose to accept them, break away from them completely, or find a way to compromise and create places where they can do both.

In her autobiographical writings, including *Fatal Flowers: On Sin, Sex, and Suicide in the Deep South* (1980), *Sleeping With Soldiers: In Search of the Macho Man* (1984), *The Woman Who Spilled Words All Over Herself: Living and Writing the Zona Rosa Way* (1997), and *Confessions of a {Female} Chauvinist* (2001), Rosemary Daniell overtly examines these choices and their repercussions. Her writings showcase her coming of age in Georgia in the 1940s and 1950s, her adulthood in the last half of the twentieth century, and a variety of insights into what Daniell perceives to be the South's attitudes toward sex, religion, and family. Particularly telling are the ways in which Daniell herself is a nexus of these southern attitudes and the ways in which these attitudes gain expression through her mingling of erotic and Christian images in both autobiographical writings and poetry, especially in her volume of (sometimes autobiographical) poems, *A Sexual Tour of the Deep South* (1975). As in all autobiographical writings, Daniell's memories seem, in part, self-constructed, self-edited and self-consciously related. Moreover, because she writes and speaks as an adult rather than a child, Daniell infuses her memories of childhood with the self-analysis of an adult, and the spaces of her childhood as they are constructed become spaces not of actual childhood, but of childhood analysis. Daniell actively creates her childhood as a place where we can view her acceptances of and (sometimes simultaneous) struggles against southern female identity. By analyzing what Daniell chooses to foreground, we can go beyond a mere rehearsing of anecdotes to seek out the reasons for her early merging of Christianity and sexuality and how these unions create a space that makes use of codified beliefs while at the same time challenging them.

During her childhood, Daniell initially turns to religion as a way to forget sexuality, as her southern culture demands. Problems arise for her when she learns that she ultimately needs to reject "sexual feelings in favor of virtue" (*Fatal Flowers* 109) because "sex, even sexual thoughts, could be a major sin, keeping [her] from God forever" (107). But young Daniell is not interested in (nor capable of) rejecting sexual feelings, and she insisted in a personal interview that as a girl she was instead "very passionate about boys and sex," and that she eventually had to sublimate her own sexual feelings by turning them into a desire for Christ and salvation. When, for example, she and her young boyfriend argue, Daniell decides to "dedicate [her] life to Jesus and try to save the lost" (109). By turning her desire for her boyfriend into a desire for Jesus, Daniell subconsciously creates a new man—one who merges the two male figures of boyfriend and Christ. This merging shows itself when Daniell reveals her childhood fantasies, including one she often had specifically while spending time in an old dump that had become her private hideaway: "I was suffused with images of Jesus that mixed with a vague sense of arms around me, of flesh rising warmly toward mine" (96). Although the dump is literally a site of the physical refuse of mankind, it is transformed through her fantasies into a space that accommodates the sacred. Her fantasies are ones of a physical melding not with her boyfriend or the latest teen heartthrob, but of Jesus. According to Daniell, these fantasies often arose because the idea of sexual desire was "tied into [her] mind, at the time, with the image of Jesus because He was such a large part of the role of goodness" (interview). The need for virtue and salvation could not destroy her sexual fantasies, but it did become a coping mechanism that molded those fantasies into something that would allow her to feel pleasure without guilt.

A similar moment appears in the work of Connie May Fowler who, as a child, believed that Jesus was her boyfriend. In her semi-autobiographical novel *Before Women had Wings*, she displaces this belief onto her protagonist, Bird, who, while suffering the effects of quick maturation forced upon her through an abusive household, finds herself imagining that Jesus is not just her friend but her boyfriend, and she is "dead certain He loved [her] special" (27). While gazing at a cheap Woolworth's image of Jesus that hangs above her bed, she considers his physical body and even imagines him watching her as she masturbates: "He was skinny, but I bet He was strong. I loved his silky, long brown hair. . . . And His eyes! They looked out upon the whole world with a loving, wise light, and I knew that they saw me in particular. He watched everything I did, knew my deepest thoughts. Even saw my unclean deeds when I touched myself in that place Mama said was named Filthy. In my daydreams, Jesus and I would walk off into a blazing sunset, holding hands. . . . in my heart of hearts, Jesus was my first boyfriend" (27).

Because of her feelings for Jesus, she is shocked and angry when her Catholic sister goes through Confirmation to become a "bride of Christ." Her mother had insisted that one of her children be Catholic like her, so although Bird is nominally Baptist, her sister is raised Catholic, which increases Bird's feeling of isolation and jealousy. As far as Bird is concerned "it wasn't fair for Phoebe to be allowed to become Jesus' bride. . . . I wanted to marry Him too" (28). By turning her thoughts away from her abusive parents and the poverty of her life and towards a Jesus who substitutes as both a loving parent and a boyfriend, Bird is able to create a place that encompasses sexuality and eroticism while still keeping her safe and "pure" in light of her growing womanhood. In fact, after she decides to "get saved," she imagines that "at any moment [she'd] be transformed into a teenager. And not just any teenager, but a young Mary Magdalene. Boys would think I was lovelier than air. But, of course, because of my saintliness, none of those fellas could so much as lay a little finger on me" (107). By imagining herself as Mary Magdalene, she constructs a self who is undeniably sexual and at the same time able to remain holy. Her desire to retain her chastity, while certainly an expectation of southern girls, seems as well to speak to the dangers inherent in the poverty and abuse around her. She wants to deny the risk of sexual activity while embodying the delights of a sexualized being. If she is Mary Magdalene, then she herself becomes a site of contested meanings both secular and sacred.

When Rosemary Daniell considers such childhood minglings later in life, she pinpoints many such instances when she combined the concepts of sexual and spiritual Eros. For example, after attending a party with her boyfriend where they fed each other grapes, the thirteen-year-old Daniell writes in her journal: "Dreamed about Jesus last night . . . had a wonderful time at the party, Troy and I fed each other" (109). The combination of a dream about Jesus and a sensuous act with her young boyfriend is a coupling that an older Daniell labels "sexuality and religiosity melted together" (108). Of course, reasons for this merging may also be found in the spaces where they occur. Church services, for example, provided a useful heterosocial environment in which to find and court potential partners during the 1940s and 1950s in the South. Daniell explains in an interview that boys would often take girls to church as "dates" and "would try to neck with girls there." She added that the boys "would cry in church and everything and then they'd go and park and try to make out." She reiterates this message in her autobiographical poem "Oh, Men!" (with it's play on "Amen"):

> At fifteen, in broader worlds,
> I found that boys from the town
> of Stone Mountain wore cowboy
> boots on dates for church,
> and after prayer, they hankered
> not for the Blood of the Lamb
> but for something similar. (27–33)

The "something similar" that these males hanker for is the penetrated bodies of southern girls, sacrificing their blood for the pleasure of the "little death." Given this scenario, it is not unlikely that southern girls (and boys for that matter) would learn to associate sex with church and religion. Margaret Wolfe explains that, in the South, "Religious services

. . . provided social outlets for young and old alike, and temptation often lurked nearby. Lusty youths particularly valued churchgoing for the assistance it lent to courting. Evening services had the additional advantage of providing them with the cover of darkness as they played the gallants escorting fair members of the opposite sex to the safety of their homes" (115). Besides providing such a space, however, churches were also highly eroticized spaces for Daniell because of the services conducted therein. During the services, she says, the singing of hymns and the communal prayers caused something that was "an ecstasy part sexual, part sacred" (109). The church services, she said, created "sexuality and religiosity melted together within the phosphorescent glow that encapsulated everything" (108).

In hindsight, this process of merging is a self-conscious one for her, and she wonders, "Did the . . . images of the Blood of the Lamb, Christ on his Cross, infest the imagination, overstimulate the genitals . . . ?" (108). Daniell's theory is provocative given the fantasies and dreams that continue to haunt her throughout her life. Perhaps the most striking of these dreams is one she has while masturbating herself to sleep as a teenager, of herself "in the arms of Jesus—or was it a brutal blond pirate?" (94). Although Daniell does not directly say so, there seems no real difference to her between Jesus and the pirate; both are manifestations of the same erotic desires. The young Daniell wants to be "sweet and nice" (74), but she also knows that nice girls do not have sex and so, as a defense against guilt, she invests her sexuality in religion (or in pirates who, much as Jesus had, were able to do as they would without the approval of society). In fact, when she fails to be a "nice" girl and spends afternoons with her boyfriend kissing, she knows that her "compulsion meant the end of . . . pure love, of [her] dreams of a baby-blue wedding . . . a Betty Crocker kitchen, and six blond children" (117). Even as a young teen, Daniell was convinced that giving in to sexual desires would lead to failure in her role as a southern woman, a role that encompasses holiness, wifehood, and motherhood, as depicted in the myriad of magazines aimed at southern women, and that, as long as she gave in to her sexual impulses, "nothing . . . could save or make [her] into a good Southern woman" (117). The only way out of such a trap may have been the creation of an imagined space where sexuality and religion did not have to be separate. In such a space, she could hear the word of God while looking at her boyfriend's picture, image, or even his very body and not worry about guilt. Thus, religion becomes inevitably linked to the same erotic feelings invoked by her sexual interest—and such feelings are only exacerbated by the services where hymns and communal prayers could heighten the physical and sensual energy in the room.

These songs and prayers that help stimulate congregants provide imagery and provoke visions that are essentially doing the same affective work as their more visual counterparts, the iconography and religious art that more often adorns Catholic churches. While visual symbols in a religious setting may help lead viewers to the "domain of the invisible," it is also true that words themselves are symbolic and the images tied to those symbols can be just as effective in creating sacred or secular spaces (or both). The images that Daniell internalizes through the Baptist hymns she hears and sings are ones of sensuality, blood, pain, ecstasy, and sacrifice. Furthermore, these hymns (still sung today) are rife with imagery of Christ as a lover, savior, and martyr. In "Just As I Am," Charlotte Elliot's hymn that Daniell often quotes, Christ is the redeemer whose "blood can cleanse" and "relieve" the poor sinner/singer. Similarly in S. Francis Xavier's "My God, I Love Thee!" Jesus is the lover who suffers and is penetrated and bleeding for his beloved: "But, O my Jesus, Thou didst me / Upon the cross embrace; / For me didst bear the nails and spear, / And manifold disgrace" (5–8). Finally, in Paul Gerhardt's "Jesus, Thy Boundless Love," singers beg Jesus to "knit my thankful heart to Thee / and reign without a rival there" (3–4). Here, the singer begs Jesus to come to his or her heart, refusing all others, and implies that Jesus is the only or supreme lover that the singer should or will ever know. Indeed, Jesus is often considered the *only* proper outlet for intense emotions. Religious historian Sandra Sizer asserts that within Protestant hymns messages were sent that "the individual by relying on Jesus achieves inward control to counter the turbulent world and his own evil passions; strength is generated internally by gaining control of emotions, turning them into positive forces by focusing them on Jesus alone" (34). These hymns thus help construct a place of sanctuary from the outside world, but also a mental focus for turning away from "evil passions" that might include Daniell's sexual desires or Bird's "unclean" acts.

This point of focus, however, may actually be less useful at getting rid of sexual passions. In these hymns, images of Jesus' crucifixion, his pain on the cross, and his redeeming blood overlap with the idea of Jesus as lover and bridegroom to create a highly sensualized, eroticized space within the church. Sizer explains how these hymns also contribute to the sense of intimacy that can heighten the emotional intensity of this space. The lyrics, she argues, convey that "[t]he secret of [Jesus'] saving power lies in a movement inward, not only toward shelter and refuge with Jesus and/or in heaven, but to a realm of intimacy" (33). In a 1978 study of hymns, sociologist Susan Tamke further explains, "Images of wounds, blood, and pain are particularly frequent in the early evangelical hymnbooks because of the evangelical emphasis on the individual's personal relationship to God through the mediation of Christ's sacrifice" (140). One such hymn, "'Praise for the Fountain Opened,'" written in 1779 by William Cowper and still included in many contemporary hymnals today, tells believers that, by bathing in the blood of Christ, or by accepting the sacrifice of Christ, they will be saved from damnation:

There is a fountain filled with blood,
> Drawn from Immanuel's veins,
And sinners, plunged beneath that flood,
> Lose all their guilty stains. (*United Methodist Hymnal* 622, lines 1–4)

This hymn, among others, is sung fairly frequently in both Baptist and Methodist churches and was undoubtedly sung by Daniell, who mentions that in church they "sang hymns about the Blood of the Lamb and what worms we were" (47). Jesus is, in this hymn, the divine presence that will save individual sinners through their intimate and individual connection not only to him, but to his blood and his wounds—symbols that bring to mind the very fleshiness and mortality of the divine Christ, his sensuality, if not his sexuality. But these wounds and the blood of Christ also symbolize something that Daniell, Fowler, and other authors would well understand—sacrifice.

Sacrifice, of course, is among the most powerful ideas in the hymns and liturgies of mainline southern Protestant denominations of the twentieth century. The idea of sacrifice is a common one for southern women, who are often taught to sacrifice their own happiness and social and erotic fulfillments for the sake of their men. But within religious arenas, sacrifice has regularly been yoked to the image of the physical body.

The most obvious images representing sacrifice, particularly in Catholic iconography, are Christ on the cross and the wounds and openings in his body. Although Baptists have rejected overt iconography associated with the crucifixion, they continue to emphasize the importance of this imagery in hymns and biblical readings. Tamke explains that "the core of the gospel message . . . was the promise of salvation brought by Christ. The Cross was, therefore, an image of overwhelming importance in evangelical hymns. Evangelical hymnbooks are filled with hymns describing the crucifixion or adoring the crucified Christ" (37). These hymns, with their "emotional intensity" and "almost amatory physiological details," allow singers not only to understand what Christ sacrificed for them, but also to relate to Christ through the act of sacrifice itself. Such relation enlarges the individual's act of sacrifice, placing it on par with the sacrifice of Jesus while at the same time making Jesus more human and thus reachable. A reachable, human Jesus becomes one who, for Daniell and other authors, is just as likely a candidate for fantasy as any popular actor or singer, and, in fact, because of the emphasis on church attendance that many of them learn, he may be an even *more* available or likely candidate.

Within both Catholic and Protestant services, sacrifice is remembered primarily through communion. Bread and wine or grape juice are ingested as symbols of Christ's body and blood, the same blood that Daniell believes she must be "washed in" (162) if she wishes to be saved. This act of communion has traditionally signified forgiveness of the member's sins, and thus the blood of Christ becomes one of the most important aspects of being saved. In Baptist ceremonies in particular, there is also an "Invitation" at the end of the sermon during which congregants are called to the front of the church to be forgiven and received into the family of Christ. During this invitation, congregants typically sing hymns that focus on the blood of Christ, and since congregants who experience conversion are met with the physical embrace of their minister and other members of the church, the body remains a central component of the experience. Crucial then in these services is the metaphorical presence of blood—signs of bodily existence—in the hymn's lyrics.

Blood, however, is another way through which women often find a connection to Jesus and, perhaps not surprisingly, references to blood proliferate in Daniell's poetry and are usually tied to sexual experience.

In "Cullasaja George," for instance, a woman thinks about dedicating her life to Christ as she performs oral sex on a man. Appropriating the words sung during Baptist Invitations and Consecrations, Daniell writes:

As speaking in tongues, her wounded lips caw
Of deliverance: a liturgy let down from the glistening labels
"FEEL OF IT SMELL OF IT TASTE OF IT jesus jesus jesus
Just As I Am, without one plea BUT THAT THY BLOOD WAS SHED." (55–59)

As the woman finishes the sexual act (an act of deliverance at that), she hears "the voice of God's man" descending "from above" to tell her, "You can get up now, sister." Furthermore, she feels "shriven of lust by lust" (62–63). The repetition of the word "jesus" in lowercase letters, perhaps signifying the moaning of the recipient of her attentions, implies that Jesus, the son of God, has been replaced by Jesus, the man. The juxtaposition of his name and the physical body of the man in the poem effectively merges the two beings into one entity, the "god-man" who is standing before the woman. As an extension of God and Christ, the man in the poem orders the woman to perform sexually for him. She, for her part, is on her knees, "praying" a "liturgy" to him. She begs for deliverance and, as she is performing oral sex, imagines herself in church, creating an imagined space where her actions, as sexual and secular as they are, can be remade as sacred. As in a communion service, she ingests the "body of Christ," or, in this case, the body of his representative; however, because she has "taken the body of Christ" into her in the form of semen from his physical surrogate, in a space which she has created as sacred, she feels clean again. The poem ends on an ironic note, with the woman driving down the mountain to Atlanta: "Behind the effortless wheel of her Triumph, / she floats down mountain toward Atlanta, sinless" (70–71). Although the Triumph in question is a car, it is also a direct reference to her success in cleansing herself of sin. It is significant, as well, that she feels triumphant while driving in her car—a space that is both solidly in place and liminally between spaces at the same time. While she is *in* the car, the car itself is literally between two fixed points or locations, and in this space, she enters into an imagined sexually sacred reality that exists while not existing.

Daniell, however, is not merely redeeming the act of sex in this and other poems by infusing it with religious significance. In fact, she seems to be doing the opposite as well. The actions performed in "Cullasaja George" combine sex and religion in a parody of religious ritual and pose a potential critique of traditional Christianity, making it "dirty." In what may be a need to rebel against the lessons taught by her mother and her society, Daniell secularizes this particular religion to diminish its power and thus separate herself from it or establish her mastery over it. But not all of the female characters in Daniell's poetry are successful in mastering their own conscience, and in "Over Chattanooga," Daniell writes of a young southern girl who "commits suicide during a ride at the county fair, driven mad by sexual guilt" (*The Woman Who Spilled Words* 131). In the poem, as the girl rides on a mechanized swing, she feels guilt because at church:

> I thought not of purity
> But the peach flesh beneath my wet white dress, of rising
> With the nipples of a siren: shivering, clearly possessed;
> How even during prayer, my eyes would fall like a witch's
> Onto the thigh of some body, my thought to what might be
> Later—no, Lord not thinking of You at all. (73–78)

Like Daniell, the girl in the poem spends her time in church watching the boys around her, thinking about the sex that might come after church, but unlike the subject of "Cullasaja George," this girl cannot find a release of the guilt—she is unable to carve out a space where the sacred and the sexual can coexist. She loosens the bar that protects her on the ride and flies out over the carnival grounds, thinking to herself that she is glad she is dying because she can save her family the disgrace of having a sexual daughter, glad that she is "saving / my Mama, my sweet baby sister from grief" (85–86). She also feels that, like Christ, she can become purified through her sacrifice and death: "this swing / on chains lifts me toward a guiltless love, a marriage" (86–87). She ends the poem with a grateful, almost ecstatic prayer to Jesus: "*Jesus, pierce my forehead / with thorns bushes whole trees: I'm coming at last*" (93–94). With her death, she has guiltlessly sexualized her meeting with Jesus, looking forward to a "marriage" with Christ. She begs him to penetrate her and with deliberate double entendre tells Jesus that she is "coming at last." Thus, her resolving of sexual frustration is paradoxically twofold: the release from sexual guilt through a death that forecloses sexual interactions, and the release of orgasm during such an interaction.

Daniell's use of penetration as both a sexual and religious metaphor is also found elsewhere in her work. In *Fatal Flowers*, she writes, "I sat in the back row with boys who tried to kiss me during the long prayers, thinking not of Hellfire and Damnation, of being Washed in the Blood, but of what might come later—of tongues, fingers, Trojans, penetration" (134). In the very next sentence she writes, "Each summer, revival meetings were held every night for two weeks to give the Holy Ghost a chance to penetrate." Whether or not the combination of the two sentences was intentional, it is telling that the same word, "penetration," is first used sexually and then religiously. The context of the word is also significant; in the first sentence, she is thinking of a man, an extension of Christ, who will penetrate her with fingers, penis, and tongue. Similarly, in the second sentence, the Holy Ghost, also an extension of Christ, is penetrative, and thus solidifies the merging of mortal man with the divine being. Penetration also shows up when Daniell is considering the nails of the Cross in her poem "Liturgy." She writes: "genuflect to One / who gave Himself / to penetration, / to mutilation" (35–38).

In his study of medieval devotional art and literature, *Closet Devotions*, Richard Rambuss illuminates a history of poetry rife with such images of Christ's penetration and mutilation and oblique references to the sensual and sexual nature of such penetration. Rambuss writes: "Through an osmosis of eroticism fueling religious affect and religiosity heightening erotic desire, devotion to Christ becomes sexualized, becomes . . . a state of the body and its passions, no less than it is an exertion of the soul. . . . This is to say that religion and sex have done, and still continue to do, each other's affective work" (101). Although many critics before Rambuss have been concerned with the physical sex of Jesus, Rambuss's interest in this nexus of sexuality and the sacred moves away from the physical manifestations of sex to sexual identity and meaning. The medieval literature and art he examines thus serve as precursors to the poems and literature now being studied.

One of the many critics and theorists whose work stands as a predecessor to Rambuss is Leo Steinberg, whose groundbreaking study of Christ's humanity, *The Sexuality of Christ in Renaissance Art and Modern*

Oblivion, examines a wealth of Renaissance images to address the question of why so many artists portrayed Christ, as both child and man, with obvious and often erect genitalia. While, unlike Rambuss's book, Steinberg's deals not at all with the *sexuality* of Christ, but only with his *sex,* i.e., his genitals, his thoughts on the physical depictions of Christ still seem short sighted. Rambuss, although he appreciates and has sympathy for Steinberg's motivations, admits that Steinberg's focus is limited by its narrow assumption that the only considerations Renaissance images "displaying [Christ's] penis" will engender are ruminations on "the doctrine of the Incarnation, the core premise of the redemptive scheme" because the penis is "the bodily site where the mystery of the Incarnation is most manifestly endowed" (61).

In other words, Steinberg does not allow for the possibility that other, less overtly religious thoughts may occur upon viewings of uncovered male loins. He argues instead that these images are an "inevitable repetitiveness" affirming that Christ "took real flesh in a woman's womb and endured [being made of flesh] until death" (71). His ultimate conclusion is that, while these images and icons "recoiled not even from the God-man's assumption of sexuality" (45), there is *no* active sexuality, or eroticism, to the Christ figure. The reason why he even *has* genitalia is to show us his humanity; to show us that, like any other man, he is susceptible to the temptations of the flesh; and, to show us that, unlike other men, he is able to rise above them. After all, "chastity consists not in impotent abstinence, but in potency under check" (17), and to show that Christ was indeed a physical *man* is to show us that he performed the ultimate sacrifice in coming *down* to mankind's level where his "chastity" can "triumph over flesh" (14). For many Christian theologians and even for some of the women in this study, that physicality or fleshiness of Christ *is* what is ultimately important because of what happens *to* that flesh—it is mortified, hurt, and sacrificed. For Daniell and Fowler, in particular, the physical suffering of Christ will eventually allow them to relate, in both good ways and bad, to Jesus.

Rather than focusing on the images themselves, however, Rambuss is concerned with the ways in which people, the medieval poets particularly, *respond* to images of Christ, be they visual images or imaginary ones. His main argument is that, even if he is not presented as a sexualized being, Christ inspires erotic thoughts, and quite often those thoughts are homoerotic as well, especially in the works of such poets as Donne and Crashaw. Daniell's work is, in many ways, a modern updating of such poetry, focusing on the same images. Although the figure of a penetrated Christ does not immediately appear sexualized, the physical sensuality of it is apparent. In Christian iconography, and especially that of Catholicism, Christ is usually depicted as a near-naked man who is penetrated, nailed to a cross, and wearing a crown of thorns while fluids drip from his forehead, hands, side and feet. Furthermore, the fluids often drip or flow along a path leading specifically towards the genitals. While the crucifix itself, with the appended body, is usually only seen in Catholic churches, many Protestant churches, including the ones Daniell attended, depict Christ this way in stained-glass images and include crosses denuded of the pierced Christ, though certainly reminiscent of him. For a child in the 1930s and 1940s, especially a female, these probably would have been the only images of an unclothed man available. Christ, under these circumstances, can provide a titillating, sensual image for young churchgoers.

Almost as if responding directly to Daniell, the preacher Billy Jack in Lee Smith's *Devil's Dream*, tells his mostly female congregation that they can't expect to find "divine love in the backseat of a Camaro" nor in the "dark night with our earthly lovers." Despite Billy Jack's exhortations, however, protagonist Katie Cocker, an award-winning musician about to release a new album of spirituals and traditional hymns, not only ends the book "saved" by Billy Jack, but also with her eye on a young bass player with whom she wishes to have a one-night stand. For Katie, music creates the kind of space where religion and sex are not necessarily at odds with one another. Ironically enough, given Billy Jack's thoughts on "the backseat of a Camaro," like the woman riding down the hill in her Triumph, Katie is a woman in constant motion—riding on her tour bus. On this bus, she is able to leave behind the demands of southern womanhood. She considers how happy it makes her to be away from her home, where she would have to go to her children's lacrosse match, take care of the house, or join in on hobbies with other society women. In fact, her ideas of a good time ("I like to dance. I will take a drink from time to time. I like to have a date" [302]), decidedly do not mesh with what her society expects of her as a good southern woman. On her tour bus, however, she can be both; although she gives up most traditional feminine duties, she also takes great pleasure in cooking for her "boys," and Katie's story ends with her getting up to soak a pot of beans. This space that has been created for and by music allows for both religious and sexual expression, neither at the expense of the other.

Not all of Lee Smith's characters, however, are as lucky as Katie Cocker. Along with her siblings, Grace Shepherd, the protagonist of *Saving Grace,* spends much of her young life traveling with her itinerant, snake-handling, preacher father and love-struck mother. During her life, she finds herself torn between sexual awakening and desires and religious teachings and traditions as laid down by first her father and then her husband. For Smith, this novel is a highly personal one. She, like Grace, spent part of her youth exploring the primitive churches of Appalachia. And, like Grace, she struggled with her attraction to mountain religion. She believes, as she says in an interview, "that the primitive church that had turned me on so much as a girl, well, they put down women," and so she still needs "to find a church that doesn't put down or stamp out things that I believe are basically good" (50). However, it is to this very church that Grace returns at the end of the novel, at the expense of her own sexual life. If Grace is returning to a church that Lee Smith herself is still struggling with, then Paula Eckard's belief that "the body and voice of the mother and the religion of the father have brought the daughter to salvation, wholeness, and a full acceptance of self" (190) may be overly optimistic. Grace's mother, during her life, is never able to escape the confines of "that primitive church." Her suicide is a direct result of the inability to find a way to develop a healthy sexuality in tandem with her religious devotion to both God and her husband. Because she never quite leaves the role of child-bride to her husband, her guilt is compounded after being seduced by her husband's son because she sees herself as an unfaithful wife, congregant, and daughter. Readers want to believe (at least this reader did) that the playful and sensual physicality of the mother can combine with the religion of the father to create a healthy heterotopic space for Grace, but without further understanding of her mother's life it may be ultimately impossible for Grace to carve out such a space, and she may end up simply returning to a way of life that killed her mother. Because Lee Smith leaves the novel open-ended, readers will of course differ in their opinions, based on Grace's journey towards what is, in essence, her moment of conversion, but to say that the book ends with Grace's sexual and sacred wholeness involves (and perhaps Lee Smith would argue that it should) a leap of faith.

Lee Smith is not unaware of the mingling of the intimacies of sex and religion. In an earlier interview, she makes it clear just how aware she is: "I do know that in my mind there has always been some link between religious intensity and sexual passion, and I mean in my growing up it was a direct link." While many psychologists, biologists, and even theologians have attempted to trace the links between religious passion and sexual passion, none can deny that they are similar in many ways and are repeatedly described using the same language. In his 1975 critical study *Passion and the Passion,* Francis Kunkel analyzes the works of several well-known authors to decide whether such a corollary exists between religious and sexual imagery and intensity. He ultimately concludes that there is no more than a "linguistic similarity," but such a statement seems unlikely in the cases of Daniell and Smith, who both see a more direct connection between the effects of each. It is in a scene of Grace at a "Homecoming" revival that we perhaps see the most obvious signs of this similarity. While singing with the congregation, she gets caught up in the feelings that drift through the crowd: "the electric lights shone on every face, making them somehow different, naked and new. I felt like I was seeing everybody for the first time, and yet I felt I'd known them all forever and ever too, as if they were part of me" (101). As the service continues, she begins to see God's breath touching the leaves around the service, and she feels "the Spirit running through me like a grass fire" (105).

While she is caught up in the noise and the smoke and the lights and the singing, she is also hearing clearly the words of her father, who is talking to her and others of the sacrifice of Jesus, of the love he feels for everyone and the power of that love. It is a heady sensation and, much like a girl caught up in a whirlwind sexual experience (as she will be later that night), Grace goes along with everyone around her, taking orgiastic pleasure from her surroundings. But much like that same girl, when the act is done, she feels "self-conscious, like I had been caught with my clothes off" (105). While in the midst of the experience, Grace experiences "naked and new" as a good sensation and a positive feeling, but once the experience is over, that same naked feeling leaves her ashamed and embarrassed. Before the shame returns, however, while she is still "swept along, carried away in the general fever of that night" (106), she agrees to a sexual rendezvous with her half-brother, Lamar. The overwhelming spiritual feelings lead to her desire to lose her virginity—the two are directly connected. Of course it can be argued that any overwhelming excitement, whatever its cause, can be sublimated into or substituted by any other excitement, but for southern girls such as Grace (and Daniell, for that matter), such excitement outside of the bounds of religion would not have been allowed, whereas such excitement in the name of religion would have been not only tolerated, but encouraged. (One is reminded here of Lee Smith's assertion that, when she was a girl, revivals had combined sexuality and spirituality into one.)

It is not, however, just in the church itself where Grace feels the commingling of sexual and religious desires. Her first experiences with sex, for example, are when she is lying in her bed listening to the sounds of snakes rattling in their boxes below her bed mixed with the sounds of her parents having sex in the next room:

> When he looked at Mama, something passed between the two of them which I didn't understand, something which scared me and made me lie restless in my bed, straining to hear them in the other room. . . . Sometimes Mama would call out in a way I could not account for.
>
> On those nights I'd lay awake for hours. . . . Sometimes I'd hear the serpents rattling in their boxes under our beds. (14)

In the Holiness communities that handle serpents, snakes are symbols of sin and evil and are thought to contain the spirits of devils. And yet they also represent the overcoming of sin, since to handle these creatures is an accomplishment over adversity that shows the power of Jesus over evil. Every night Grace falls asleep listening to the sounds of serpents "rattling in their boxes" under her bed, reminding her of the wages of sin (the bite of the serpent); the combination of the sounds of sex and snakes seems to lead Grace to simultaneous equations of sex with sin, and with the overcoming of sin. Those "restless" nights represent Grace's earliest sexual yearnings, and by associating the sounds of those serpents with the sounds of sex during these moments, Grace subconsciously creates a place in her bedroom where religion and sex are one.

In his "Witches and Jesus: Lee Smith's Appalachian Religion," published in the *Southern Literary Journal,* Conrad Ostwalt makes a similar discovery in studying another of Smith's novels, *Black Mountain Breakdown,* alongside her short story, "Tongues of Fire." Both of these works, he says, allow for "the empowering possibilities of religious feeling" and the "spiritualization of sexuality" (113). Like Grace, Crystal Spangler, the heroine of *Black Mountain Breakdown* and Karen in "Speaking in Tongues" both attend revivals and charismatic church services. And, also like Grace, both of these characters experience a kind of sensual overload associated with the religious fervor of the event/service. Crystal, as Ostwalt also points out, feels, when religiously excited, the same way she does when she is with her boyfriend: "alive, fully alive and fully real, more than real" (126).[1] In Karen's case, it even leads to speaking in tongues—something that Grace herself also does. One scene, however, that Ostwalt does not include in his analysis of this story is the scene when Karen first comes to believe that there is something special about religion. While attending a traditional Methodist service with her grandparents, Karen, in a scene reminiscent of Daniell's earlier description, sees the visiting preacher combined with the light of the stained-glass windows above him, and begins to feel her heart thumping rapidly as she stares at the man who looks to her "like an angel": "probably the Angel Gabriel, because of his curly blond hair. And he was so *young*—just out of seminary, somebody said after the service. It was a warm fall Sunday, and rays of colored light shot through the stained-glass windows at the side of the church to glance off Johnny Rock Malone's pale face. 'He *walks* with me, and He *talks* with me,' we sang. My heart started beating double time" (80). Although Karen has, until this point, been "interested in religion," it is only when the image/words of God are mediated through this mortal man (literally, as the light shines through the window only to glance off of him) that it moves her and makes her feel "wild and trembly" inside (81). And later, when she seeks out this same experience in a countryside Holiness church, she finds that same joy in listening to the parishioners speak in tongues.

Ostwalt argues that it is this ability to grasp the sensual language of religion that allows Karen to avoid the "paralysis and inability to speak" that Crystal suffers at the end of *Black Mountain Breakdown.* But Crystal suffers from more than just an inability to find a voice—because of her

rape at the hands of her mentally disturbed uncle, she is unable to find
a space where the truth of her sexuality can combine with any kind of
spirituality. When she is at church, she may feel the same way she feels
when her boyfriends touch her, but in this case, she has created a space
not of combination, but of exclusion. Religious ecstasy and physical
ecstasy are both escapes for her, but she is unable to combine them to
make a healthy space. In the end, she retreats physically to her bedroom
on Black Mountain, the only place where, once, everything had been
clear cut, and mentally to the space of her mind, although Smith does
not allow us (nor anyone else) into that space—it is, as mentioned, ex-
clusionary. The heterotopic spaces that Daniell carves out for herself,
or that Karen is able to create in "Tongues of Fire" are inclusionary and
allow for the expression of both religious and sensual/sexual feelings.
The space in which we leave Crystal is not a created space, but a space
of retreat, a place where she is retreating both in the sense of *going
backwards* and *hiding away.* And the window that opens out onto the
mountain, and through which we may view Crystal, serves the purpose
of emphasizing her separation from the rest of the world, giving the
bedroom the cloistered feeling of a convent, keeping her in the care of
her female friend Agnes and away from the demands, both mental and
physical, of being part of the human race.

If Crystal's bedroom effectually equates her with a cloistered nun,
then Claire, a young novitiate in Valerie Martin's *A Recent Martyr,* provides us a southern woman who *actively* seeks out such separation from
the rest of the world. Having been sent away from her convent for a
year before taking her vows, Claire creates, in her own bedroom, a sacred space where she can combine a physical sensuality with a feeling
of heightened spiritual awareness. By replicating the sparse space of her
convent cell, she turns her bedroom into a prayer closet where she can
alternately pray quietly or mortify her flesh with a cat o' nine tails as
relief for a very real and physical frustration. But the space she creates in
her bedroom is a mental space as well as a physical one. In her "cell like
bedroom" (98), after praying and staring up at the crucifix that hangs on
her wall (one of the few decorations in the room), she imagines "that she
was equipped to make the long journey that would end in a union with
her Creator" (47). Before she can find such a union, however, she knows
she must find a way to bring herself closer to him because she isn't sure

"just how far in which direction she had drifted in the night." Though she is afraid that her own dreams may take her *away* from Christ, she is sure that she "kn[ows] a sure cure for this difficulty in concentrating"—and so she whips herself with a leather strap. As she does, she forces herself to imagine the "greeting the angel gave to Christ's Virgin Mother" when he came to tell her of her impending motherhood and to, presumably, impregnate her as a proxy for God. Once she is done hurting herself, she goes down on her knees, falling back on her haunches in a rigid, tight, almost painful position and sighs, "Ah, I love you. I love you," like a satisfied lover. And when she finally is able to "[come] to herself . . . her legs were cramped and she crawled on hands and knees to a chair" where she is able to get dressed. Like a lover who has just been with her beloved, she is undressed, in her bedroom, physically exhausted, and sighing in a pleasured exhaustion, telling him how much she loves him, before relaxing her cramped legs and getting up to put her clothes back on.

What makes this scene from *A Recent Martyr* more compelling is that in another of Martin's novels, *Set in Motion,* a similar scene is enacted during the course of a sexual tryst as opposed to a prayer session. Helene Thatcher, a New Orleans social worker who lives a promiscuous life, hoping sex will allow her to connect with people, has a sexual affair with her friend's fiancé, a domineering and powerful man she imagines as looking like "the sun" (70). During the sex, she has a vision wherein she "experience[s] the sensation of being flooded by a kind of light, like water, and being open to this flood, although it was blinding, because it was blinding" (126). And when the sex is done, she feels "dazed and disheveled, defenseless," and is unable to move until she returns to herself and is able to pull her dress back on. The two scenes, so similar in structure and tone, allow Martin to envision a kind of mystical experience where the boundaries between the sacred and the sexual are rubbed thin, if not completely rubbed out. In each scene, the bedroom becomes a place where physical pleasure (and pain) can take on spiritual overtones so that a man (Helene's friend's fiancé) may become a savior and where the savior becomes a man whose earthly identity is confirmed by his mortal mother.

A Recent Martyr's Claire has a number of other visions throughout the novel, but one of the most interesting occurs not while in her bedroom, but in church. This vision is not of the Virgin Mary; instead it is of suffering and penetration that further identifies Christ as both a mortal and as her lover. While praying in front of a crucifix, she imagines "Christ's hand as it closed about the shank of the impending nail." She falls almost comatose, and when she is startled awake by her confessor, Father Paine, she lies, saying that she must have fainted. In response to his skepticism, she admits that she had had a vision of "'his hand'" (99). What she realizes from this vision and her other visions, however, is "that her Lover wanted more than her service. He wanted her entirely; He wanted her soul for His own and His desire was not diminished by her fear of being owned" (99–100). It is only following this vision of pain and penetration, similar to the one she has earlier in the bedroom, that Claire directly refers to Jesus as her lover. The difference is that, in the bedroom, she cries out her love for him, and in the Church, she realizes that he too wants her. The two scenes blend together to create a relationship in which Jesus is a reciprocal lover who is not only passively adored, but actively adoring (and demanding).

Pascal, Claire's would-be lover, questions the mutuality of Claire's relationship with Jesus by insisting that religious ecstasy is more "like masturbation," but Claire counters that it's only masturbation for *him* because he believes himself "to be utterly alone" (63), emphasizing her belief that during her bouts of ecstasy she is accompanied by Jesus. He later makes a similar comment when he cuttingly (and perhaps insightfully) comments upon Claire's act of praying by asking her, "And your hands . . . I've no doubt you'll have them in your lap?" (111). Even though Claire finds his question to be "obscene," she is unable and unwilling to stop her next vision in the cathedral, one that happens only moments after she has spoken to Pascal. As she listens to Scarlatti's *Stabat Mater,* she begins to think about "the Mother of Christ as she stood beneath the cross on which her only Son hung in agony, still conscious, His divine eyes fixed on her" and then tries to banish "everything but the mental picture of Christ's suffering," while digging her nails into her palms. "She thought of His hands, how the broken nerves and flesh must have throbbed from the shock of the nails. Her throat contracted and from it issued a sigh, almost inaudible, such as escapes with the onset of anticipated pain" (113). And, just as in her earlier vision, this one begins not with images of Christ, but of Christ's mother. Perhaps Mary's motherhood reminds her of the role she will never play as a nun—a role that requires, outside of God's direct edict, sexual activity. Despite Mary's continuing virginity, however, Claire cannot stay focused on Mary as a role model, and she turns her thoughts to the suffering Jesus. She is unable, ultimately, to relate to Mary, the woman and mother, the way she is able to relate to Jesus in his pain.

It is only through suffering, in fact, that Claire is able to relate to the world at all. When Claire later confesses to Father Paine her inability to relate to people, her confessor tells her that he is afraid she "didn't possess a generous heart" (132), and she realizes he is right—she is only able to offer sacrifice and suffering, not love. She has internalized at least some of the rules that her society has placed on women—she is willing to sacrifice even unto the mortification of her very flesh, but she is unable to open herself up to connect with others. As she tries to figure out why, she considers that perhaps the Lord "made her to be something she hadn't the courage to be; He had made her to engage her heart, but she withheld her heart" (132). That she means he had made her a *woman* and that she is unable to be a good one become clear when she tells Father Paine that what she fears is not only love, but being female:

> ". . . you have the strength I never had and you can do better."
> "And what could be better?"
> The priest was silent.
> "Being a wife?" she said contemptuously. "Being a mother? Being a banker, a political woman?"
> Still he didn't speak.
> "My options are limited, Father," she said. "I'm a woman."
> "And you want to be a saint," he said.
> . . . "Yes," she said, nodding and smiling through a vision that threatened to blur with tears. "Oh, yes." (135)

By becoming a saint, Claire hopes to transcend the state of "womanhood" and become something more. It is unsurprising, once readers are aware of Claire's desire for sainthood, that she is unable to stay focused on images or visions of Mary and instead finds both physical and spiritual pleasure in the suffering of Christ—a mortal male.[2]

It's worth mentioning the similarities between Claire and Emma, the other woman in *A Recent Martyr*, and their desires for a union with the divine. In many ways, Emma stands as Claire's doppelganger. Like Claire, she contemplates the convent as a young girl, but unlike Claire, she gives up the appeal of religion for the reality of the sensual world. And now, as an adult, Emma is seeking in her physical relationship with her lover (as opposed to her husband) the same kind of ecstatic experience that Claire seeks through her relationship with God. Unlike Claire, however, Emma elevates her all-too-real worldly lover to the role of the divine. Her methods, feelings, and desires, however, are incredibly similar to Claire's. Instead of self-flagellation, she relies on Pascal to hurt her, pushing him further and further in their sadomasochistic sex games, sure that some day he will kill her, but welcoming such intensity. She feels she is "ready to go beyond the limitations of [her] senses if only [she] could take him with [her]" (138). She believes that "there is something to be said for a lover with whom one can be united *only* in death," and when she sees Pascal above her, she cannot stop thinking of "Claire's determination to have her spiritual Lover." Still, she finds herself "divinely fortunate to have found" Pascal, whose very presence makes her feel like a supplicant before her divinity.

Like Daniell in her forays to the trash dump, Emma creates, in every secret place where she meets her lover—be it his apartment, a hotel room, or a bar—a place of worship where she finds pleasure through the act of sacrificing her desires to him. And, like Claire, this sacrifice gives her physical pleasure. She risks her marriage, her child, even her career, just to give herself to him over and over. Through this sacrifice, and by creating a space in which Pascal becomes divine, she realizes that she has found "what Claire said she wanted . . . a lover who would consume me entirely" (167). This desire for consummation may look, on the surface, like nothing more than unhealthy masochism, but what it masks for both of these women is a desire for connection and transcendence that Simone de Beauvoir discusses in *The Second Sex,* particularly in the sections "The Mystic," and "The Woman in Love." A desire for consummation, or annihilation, she argues, can only be called masochism, which for her implies a hatred of the self, when "the consciousness of the subject is directed back toward the ego to see it in a humiliating position" (650). Because neither Claire nor Emma finds her own bodily desires humiliating, and because neither of them turns her desires against herself, their masochism, their wish to transcend the flesh and body, the here and now, seems less like self-hatred. Both of these women are able to create an imagined space where the sexual and the sacred are not at odds, no matter how "obscene" Claire may, on the surface, believe such a space to be.

It is perhaps an escape from obscenity that drives Bone, the main character in Dorothy Allison's *Bastard Out of Carolina,* to create for herself multiple spaces where sex, fantasy, and spirituality can combine to protect her from the psychic dangers of her stepfather Glen's sexual and physical abuse. While many critics have excelled at examining the crucial aspects of "white trash" culture that Allison explodes in this novel, and most of them deal at least cursorily with the masturbatory fantasies of violence and anger that help fuel Bone's growing strength, few of them deal with Bone's burgeoning search for spirituality or how that search adds to her strength through the creation of safe spaces (both real and imagined) wherein she can nurture that growth. In her essay "Controlling Images in Dorothy Allison," Katherine Henninger points out that, while Bone's first response to being sexually abused by Glen is silence, "her second, sub-conscious, response is to reconfigure the trauma in a fantasy of fire, to which she masturbates and orgasms. As the abuse continues, her daydream metamorphoses into a more potent fantasy of being watched as Glen beats her, the captive watchers admiring her courage and defiance and hating Glen" (99). These fantasies of intense pain (including fire and beatings) and being watched are powerful ways to re-imagine her abuse in order to begin to overcome it, but it is not only during masturbation that she has these fantasies of intensity and exhibitionism—they occur in church as well.

When Bone decides that she needs to find salvation, it is in part because of the attention that being saved will bring her. She believes, as her uncle has told her, "if you were not saved, not part of the congregation, you were all anyone could see at the invocation. There was something heady and enthralling about being the object of all that attention" (151). As a result, she wants "the church to fill up with everyone I knew. I wanted the way I felt to mean something and for everything in my life to change because of it" (152). Just as having people watch her being beaten make her the heroine and Glen the villain in a story that she can control, having people watch her get saved will make her life "change" in presumably positive ways. By making herself the object of other people's gazes, she manages a twofold salvation—she can escape the guilt she carries for her own abuse, and she can make others witness to the abuse, sharing her responsibility for what happens. The church, then, becomes the type of heterotopic site that Foucault calls "compensatory." It is a site that has "a function in relation to all the space that remains" in order to "create a space that is other, another real space, as perfect, as meticulous, as well arranged as ours is messy, ill constructed, and jumbled" (27). Bone's life is definitely "messy, ill constructed, and jumbled," and so church becomes the place in which all wrongs can be made right, all mess can be made ordered, through the mutual powers of seeing and telling. If the church fills up with people who see her salvation, who see her bring perfection to her life, then the church will be a space in which the reality of her life has no place.

Church services and the desire for salvation also bring her a hunger for spiritual pain that is similar to her hunger for intensity during masturbation: "I wanted, I wanted, I wanted something—Jesus or God or orange-blossom scent or dark chocolate terror in my throat. Something hurt me, ached in me" (151). What both of these spaces—the spaces of church and of violent fantasy—have in common is that they are spaces where, even if she is being beaten, she is still ultimately safe. Because of this need for safety, even though Bone eventually gives up her quest for religious salvation, she does not give up her need for spirituality. What she turns to is the same thing that many of Lee Smith's characters turn to—gospel music. When she begins listening to gospel, what she hears is more than just adoration: "I heard . . . the desperation swelling rough raw voices, the red-faced men and pale sweating women moaning in the back pews. . . . Moaning and waiting, waiting and praying, 'to be washed, *Lord Jesus!* Washed in the blood of the Lamb!' The hunger, the lust, and the yearning were palpable. I understood that hunger as I understood nothing else, though I could not tell if what I truly hungered for was God or love or absolution" (148).

Even though Bone gets firsthand knowledge that gospel singers drink, have sex, and engage in other "sinful" activities, she finds in the space of the music a place where those behaviors are not definitive. In fact, when she later hears a woman singing as part of a choir in a black, country church, she is finally able to articulate just how much gospel music combines the secular and the sacred: "Gut-shaking, deep-bellied, powerful voices rolled through the dried leaves and hot air. This was the real stuff. I could feel the whiskey edge, the grief and holding on, the dark night terror and determination of real gospel" (169). Gospel includes, for Bone, the intensity of her most violent fantasies along with the spiritual yearning of the most fervent religious believers. Bone's movement between religious fantasies (being saved, being a gospel singer) and sexual ones provides multiple outlets for her yearnings, the yearnings for safety and escape from the obscenity of Glen's abuse and her own sense of shame.

Bone, however, isn't Allison's only character who manages to carve out a space that represents both the erotic and the spiritual as a place of safety. In Allison's 1999 *Cavedweller,* Cissy, the daughter of formerly famous musicians, moves away from Los Angeles with her mother to her mother's rural hometown of Cayro, Georgia, after her drinking and drug-abusing father dies. Cissy's existence in Cayro, much like her mother's, is a difficult one as she learns to adjust to a rural setting and meets the daughters and first husband that her mother had left behind. Dealing with the normal fears and desires of adolescence, Cissy must also learn to cope for the first time with being labeled, like Bone, "trash." Ultimately it is through exploring the local caves that Cissy is able to create a holistic space where she can become both a spiritual and a sexual being. In her essay "'Excavated from the Inside': White Trash and Dorothy Allison's *Cavedweller,*" Karen Gaffney looks at the way that Cissy's discovered love of cave exploration helps Cissy come to terms with "her position at the intersection of race, class, gender, and sexual orientation" (51). I would, however, add religion to this intersection as well. Deep in the caves, completely surrounded by darkness, Cissy imagines the cave as "female . . . the dark was female and God was dark" (276). Although Cissy's God is a feminine one, as opposed to a Christian one, she still configures the deity as a sensual one in whose presence, as Gaffney writes, she can "voice her queer identity" and her "female sexuality" (56). Cissy's configuration of the cave as a space of the female and motherly divine allows this very real space of exclusion to become, for Cissy, a space of *inclusion.* Here, although mostly excluded from others, she is able to find her sexuality through exposure to the divine, and to incorporate herself better into a society that she has heretofore seen as isolating.

And finally, Ninah, the protagonist of Sheri Reynolds's *Rapture of Canaan* provides an illuminating counterpoint to the previous examples and showcases what Rene Girard may mean when he argues that, in mediated desires, "the mediator's prestige is imparted to the object of desire and confers upon it an illusory value. Triangular desire is the desire which transfigures its object" (*Deceit* 17). By imagining that Jesus not only approves of her having sex with her boyfriend, but is also present in their sex act, Ninah makes the act of sex a sacred one that is elevated, along with her boyfriend James, to the level of holiness. When these acts ultimately result in Ninah's pregnancy, she then convinces herself that the child must also be holy and she herself a modern Virgin Mary.

Unlike the characters who live in a secular world and create spaces for themselves that allow them to forge room for the sacred, Ninah lives in a community that is already supposedly holy. The Holiness Pentecostal religious community in which she lives is a strict one, run by her grandfather Herman and centered on the Church of Fire and Brimstone and God's Almighty Baptizing Wind. The community's laws are based not only on the laws of the Bible, but also upon the laws determined by Herman. While he uses parts of the Bible in creating his laws, he uses "only the parts he liked" and then comes up with new laws whose sources are known only to him. Taking as her inspiration such books as *The Irish Penitentials* and *The Medieval Handbooks of Penance,* Sheri Reynolds creates in Herman an almost inquisitional Pentecostal preacher whose iron fist, according to his own wife (Ninah's "Nannah"), has "a grip so hard it could strangle a person if he weren't careful" (110). Laws that set punishments for everything from stealing grapes to wearing makeup to adultery are significant in that they control not only the spiritual concerns of the community, but the social and ethical ones as well. By choosing which of the laws to include and which to exclude, Herman becomes the sole authority of what is and isn't socially acceptable in the Fire and Brimstone community, and, as might be expected, the laws he chooses to include dovetail nicely with many of the unwritten southern "laws" regarding religion, work, gender, and the relationships between people.

On the surface, the community, with its strange rules and outdated punishments, is very different from the southern communities that surround it. The Fire and Brimstone community doesn't believes in doctors; its members aren't allowed to watch television, wear makeup, cut hair, or buy clothes at stores in town. The women do not wear jewelry or clothes that will emphasize their curves, and they do not participate in social gatherings outside of their small community. There are no "debutante balls" for young women, and dates, with the exception of church dates, are practically forbidden; however, these surface differences are merely that—surfaces. Underneath the cut hair and homemade clothes, the members, especially the women, of the community, adhere to a larger set of southern guidelines that are inescapable even by those who attempt escape.

Women, just as Daniell learned in her own mainstream southern community, are expected to be the more holy of the community, and just as Daniell learned when her husband blamed her for his own failure to be saved, if a man "backslides," the female is blamed for his fall, since she is supposed to be the one keeping him upright. When, for example, Ninah confronts her boyfriend James with her pregnancy, James tells her, "The Devil comes to man in the shape of a woman. I knew that. But I didn't think it'd be *you*" (158). One of the most potent similarities between the women in the holiness community and women outside of such a tight-knit, religious group, however, is the way in which female sexuality is condemned and female religious ecstasy is condoned and encouraged. Ninah's sister and other females in the community are often praised for their passionate embrace of the Holy Spirit during church services, and speaking in tongues is common primarily among the females of the congregation. In fact, the ecstasy that she sees on the faces of those women who participate in glossolalia, while a common sight, begins to make Ninah feel uncomfortable the closer she gets to sexual maturity, and the more she begins to feel "flutters" for James.

With the onset of sexual awakening, Ninah begins to believe that speaking in tongues at first feels "like something she should do somewhere else. Not in church" (45). Ninah's burgeoning sexuality allows her to see and understand that there is something about the excitement of spiritual possession that is at least somewhat similar to the sexual excitement that she is beginning to feel. As she sits next to James and watches her sister and others experience religious ecstasy, she begins to wonder if perhaps she might find such ecstasy somewhere other than in church: "I was embarrassed that God had never shared with me his language, had never given me his special words, his almighty baptizing wind. / And I was embarrassed to think that I might find it in some other place" (45). Despite her embarrassment, or perhaps because of it, she is drawing a correlation between religious ecstasy and other forms of ecstasy, although it is only later, when she is sitting in front of James on a horse, feeling sexual stimulation from her closeness to him, that she starts to realize firmly that there *are* other forms of ecstasy. James's touch makes her forget her plans to go exploring with the other children; instead, she "was too busy trying to memorize the way James' legs felt around my backside, hanging on"; and although she tries to tell herself "it was no different from sitting next to him in church" (46), she realizes that there is something more to what she is feeling that will change how she responds to the church community as well as to James.

The connection between religious and sexual ecstasy only intensifies once Ninah begins to have sex with James. Ninah and James together create a situation and a space in which Jesus does not only endorse their behavior, he participates in it. Ninah is expected, as a condition of being "good," to deny her sexuality. After Ninah and James become prayer partners, however, the relationship between the two of them becomes fraught with sexual feelings. The prayer sessions take place in Ninah's home, and sometimes during these meetings, Ninah is acutely aware that her parents are also doing something other than praying in their back bedroom: "and sometimes I'd hear Mamma and Daddy crying out and panting, and I'd wonder if they were really praying at all. That secret blushing that goes on inside your skin would fill me up, fill me red and sweet, like exotic fruit from India, and I'd grip James' hand tighter, hoping he'd feel it too" (90). James not only feels it, however, he capitalizes on the emotional intensity that is an allowable religious expression if not a sexual one. When Ninah asks Jesus to help "me and James to know your love, to be able to share with each other your love," James repeats her request, but he manipulates the language to say something different: "Let me love Ninah for you, oh Jesus. Let me be the one to show her your love" (94). Although Ninah is aware that his request "might be a tiny bit different," she is excited by it nonetheless, for here is a way to express her sexuality without feeling the guilt of being "bad."

She allows herself to be swept up in James's requests to Jesus from then on. As long as they are involved in religious worship, such ecstasy is not only permitted, but encouraged, just as the passionate glossolalia had been in church, and so Ninah is able to excuse and enjoy her sexual experiences as being divinely inspired. In fact, when she is filled with the kind of fervor she had seen in her sister in church, she assumes that, if Jesus is the one who can cause such a feeling, that James "must be Jesus himself" (123). If Jesus is their Girardian mediator, allowing them to come together without guilt, then James is the object, elevated to the holy. While Ninah is a smart girl, and although there are some hints that she knows what she and James are doing is not having sex with Jesus, she manages to convince herself of it well enough to extend her faith in her relationship with James to other relationships that have been deemed sinful. Ben Harback, a member of the community, is punished for having an affair with a woman from another religious community, and after she begins having sex with James, Ninah reconsiders this punishment: "I couldn't help wondering if maybe in secret, Ben Harback prayed with Corinthian the way that I prayed with James. Because if that was the case, whether she was a backslidden Holiness or not didn't matter. That kind of praying was outside the realm of judgment" (124). Ninah is now questioning everything she has been taught, but by convincing herself that she is engaged in the work of Jesus, she doesn't have to feel guilty about it. She has created a place where guilt is irrelevant because, like her "praying" with James, it is "outside the realm of judgment."

Ninah eventually becomes aware of her own participation in the creation of this space when she consciously *pretends* to be speaking to Jesus in order to convince James they should continue having sex after he expresses doubts. She pretends that Jesus has suddenly spoken to her and asked that she give a ring to James to indicate that they are married (the only situation that would allow them to continue having sex without guilt). Unfortunately, because she is aware that she is pretending, it is impossible for her to feel that there is anything special or mystical in the situation, and she wonders if it has been a lie all along. That sudden knowledge fills her with dread, even as it provides James with all the excuse he needs: "And then James was on top of me again, but it was different—because I knew it was James and not Jesus. I didn't feel glowing and holy afterwards. I felt like I was made from mud. . . . I prayed for the ceiling to fall right in on me and flatten my face and scar me up so that nobody, not James, not Jesus, not anybody at all would ever want to touch me again" (149). Even though James is happy, Ninah is miserable and feels eaten up by guilt. She also wonders if Jesus has left their unions *because* she lied, and she no longer finds the sex pleasurable. Ninah's feelings confirm that in a space, be it real or imagined, where sex exists without a connection to spirituality, neither of them function properly and there is no pleasure to be found in either. And with this knowledge, she decides that she will attempt to reconnect to her spirituality by going to church and actively speaking in tongues.

Unlike Lee Smith's Grace, Ninah is consciously choosing to represent herself as speaking in tongues, and to use that glossolalia to recreate a place where religious and sexual ecstasy come together. While in church, she gets to her feet and begins to chant "hebamashundi," the only sound that she can remember from other people having spoken in tongues in church. Perhaps because she wants it so badly, she loses control of her own words and falls into what may be a self-induced trance:

> Then I knew I was going to pass out. I was almost certain. I felt sick and weak and carried away. As far as I could tell, God wasn't leading me anywhere. I was making the words up as I went, and they seized up in my mouth and spilled like lies all over the hard wood floor. . . . Around the church, there was the sound of whoops and Amens and clapping and the strange words that I was making up, making up, and everything was dark on either side of me, but right up front, where Grandpa Herman stood, beckoning me with his arms, it was bright for a second, and then that was gone too and I was sitting back down, out of breath, convulsing inside. (153)

Even though Ninah knows she is making up the words, there is definitely a sense of the mystical to this scene as everything seems to speed up, light goes in and out, and her own words seem to take control of her tongue. For days after this event, she walks around repeating the word "hebamashundi," using it almost as an anchor when she begins to feel disconnected. Even though the word is a lie, it seems to keep her rooted to reality and to clear a path in her mind through which she can stay connected to a new spirituality, a new relationship that she develops with Jesus when, shortly after, she realizes she is pregnant.

After the realization of her pregnancy, Ninah convinces herself that what she and James had been doing was, indeed, holy—and that the baby inside of her, rather than being James's baby, is actually Jesus'. During her prayer times with James, she closes her eyes, whispering "hebamas-hundi" over and over again, thinking "maybe it *was* Jesus' baby—because if we hadn't been sinning and had only been knowing Jesus through each other, then it couldn't be anything *but* Jesus'" (157). But when she imagines Jesus, it's a new Jesus—one who visits her during the night from his cross, holding out azaleas—the flower Herman had used to court his wife—for her. While Jesus still makes her think of the mystical, pleasurable experiences she had with her lover, he now also makes her think of the authoritarian regime set up by her grandfather in his name. He is both the ultimate patriarchal penal figure and the most tender of forgiving lovers. Ninah finds a physical manifestation of this combination when she later insists that James make love to her even though he is wearing a belt of barbed wire around his waist as punishment for his sins. They have sex while he's wearing the belt, and she insists that he move "harder . . . to know Jesus' pain" (163). Ninah, like Martin's Claire, is able to relate to Jesus through his pain, and to combine physical gratification with spiritual enlightenment through her own.

After James commits suicide out of guilt and her community forces her into seclusion as punishment for her sins, Ninah is literally trapped in one physical space, and her imagined spaces become even more important to her survival. In a fascinating twist, she begins to decorate both her physical space and her imagined ones with rugs. Through the act of weaving rugs, Ninah is able to begin to combine all of the elements of her life. Threads from the rope with which James committed suicide go into her rugs, as do bits of barbed wire, threads from James's clothes and, after she gives birth, blood from her son's birthing. Ninah creates a literal, physical manifestation of the combination of spiritual and secular that has heretofore remained only imagined. She combines the mundane, the everyday, the sexual, the spiritual, and even life and death into these rugs of hers, trying to tell more and more stories. These rugs and their stories ultimately allow Ninah to see the connections in her life as real things, to see the truth of her relationships and her desires for both James and Jesus. But if her rugs are a physical symbol of Foucault's heterotopic space, they are also an example of Mikhail Bakhtin's heteroglossia, with numerous voices and cultural conditions speaking through the art itself. They speak of her sacred and social duties, but also of southern and religious etiquette, fears, pains, and desires. Ninah's earlier pretentions to glossolalia are a first attempt at finding a personal voice that encompasses all of her contradictory thoughts and desires, but the space of the church, with its codified rules and masculine leadership, leaves her unfulfilled. The rugs, on the other hand, allow for multiple, contradictory expressions, and they themselves are the heterotopic space that allows for such communication.

Her son, Canaan, is another such physical symbol. Because Canaan is born with his hands fused together, the community refuses to see him as a boy and instead sees him as a symbol of the divine. Ninah eventually, against the ordinance of her community, cuts his hands apart in order to make it clear that, even if he contains the divine within him, he must also be seen as human. He may be a Christ figure, but if he is, he is the Christ who is man as well as divine. His humanity is *important,* not just something to be dismissed. Like the figure of Jesus himself, Canaan exists in a space that contains both the sacred and the secular—and was created through a combination of both. Herman and the rest of the community want to see Canaan as a figure who will change the world—and he is. But the changes that he creates will move the community away from the austere, authoritarian nature of Herman's religion and toward a more holistic faith that incorporates both the physical and the divine.

One commonality of all of these female characters is that their lives as children are *not* holistic. Sexuality and spirituality are separated and departmentalized. As southern apologist Lillian Smith says, girls growing up in the South are taught that all things sexual are shameful, that all things religious are good, and that even "curiosity about [the body] is not good" (89). Through cultural conditioning, these girls learn that they must strive for holiness, that they must sacrifice to be truly good, and that they must deny all sexual passion. On the other hand, they are also taught that religious passion is not only condoned, it can get them noticed and even revered. For girls who often feel invisible (Bone, Bird, Ninah, and others), such attention is, as Bone says, "heady and enthralling." In particular, many of these girls seek out attention from an otherwise disapproving community. It is, however, too reductive to simply say that these girls are attention seeking, especially in the light of the private, heterotopic spaces they create to foster strength and wholeness. Instead, the attention that they receive often fills a need that may otherwise be ignored—they turn to religion when they are sublimating sexual desires, or turn to sex as a way of finding what they once found with religion. When they are able to move beyond the either/or of such a scenario, however, and find spaces that can contain and incorporate contested and often opposing meanings, what they do goes beyond mere sublimation and becomes, like Ninah's rugs, a whole new (and whole) creation.

CHAPTER 3

Resolving the Parental Conflict

> Sometimes, I become her child, trusting, taking in everything she says.
> Her flesh, her body, her lust and hunger—I believe. I believe, and it is
> not a lie.
> —DOROTHY ALLISON, "Her Body, Mine, and His"

The heterotopic space containing sexuality, the sacred, and the South
becomes necessarily more complicated with the addition of parental
conflicts. Certainly there is a rich narrative history of southern girls who
"rebel" against their parents, throwing off or at least struggling with the
cultural teachings of their family and society. Rosemary Daniell spent
years fighting what she sees as the southern enculturation of girls, Lee
Smith's females struggle against what Rebecca Smith calls "a backdrop of
the myth of Southern womanhood," and Connie May Fowler and Dorothy Allison had to overcome parental neglect and abuse stemming from
what they see as the effects of southern tradition on their own parents.
From amongst our fictional girls, there is a plethora of Lee Smith characters who deal not only with the lessons taught them by parents, but with
the parents themselves, many of them neglectful, abusive, and/or absent.
For some of these girls, the conflicts they encounter between parents/
parental teachings and their personal spaces of the sexual and sacred are
resolved in what appear to be incestuous ways. In Smith's *Saving Grace*,
for example, Grace is sexually attracted for the first time to a boy who is
not only related to her, but also a dead ringer both physically and emotionally for her neglectful preacher father, and Daniell's conflict with
her mother and her mother's teachings regarding etiquette and religion

resolves itself incestuously in a literal bisexuality. For others of these characters, resolution can only be had by sublimating and/or substituting one for the other. Murmur Lee, the epileptic child of an emotionally distant, religious woman in Fowler's *The Problem with Murmur Lee,* for example, reinvents her epilepsy as fits of religious ecstasy that allow her to momentarily connect with her mother. And Bird, the daughter of an abusive, alcoholic mother in Fowler's autobiographic novel *Before Women Had Wings,* envisions her mother as a cruel, Old Testament God and Jesus as a young boyfriend who initially helps her not only to recreate her relationship with religion, but to escape the capriciousness of her mother. Such conflicts and their resolutions are unavoidable in a culture where family is at the very heart of all teachings, but where the lessons passed down are always conflicting and often repressive.

While it is useful to remember Freud's connection to theories of the sexualized relationship between parents and children, the struggles of the characters in these texts go beyond the rehashing of Oedipal identity formation. However, one text whose analysis benefits from the work of both Freud and Jacques Lacan is Connie May Fowler's most recent novel, *The Problem with Murmur Lee.* Murmur Lee, who narrates portions of the book posthumously, is the product of rape, and her mother, though she is not physically abusive towards her child, seems unable to forget the traumatic cause of her pregnancy. Burying herself in Catholic religious worship, she spends more time in prayer or in church than she does with her family, and the man that Murmur Lee knows as her father (she is not aware of the rape until after her own death) is equally neglectful, keeping himself away from his family for the most part. Even in her childhood, Murmur Lee is aware and resentful of the religion that she believes keeps her mother from her, thinking to herself that "Mother loved Christ more than she loved me" (73). Drawing upon the work of Lacan, we can see that religion has become the symbolic Father in this family in a classically Oedipal situation, keeping Murmur Lee away from intimacy with her mother. Murmur Lee is also an undiagnosed victim of a rare form of epilepsy (musicogenic) brought on, in her case, by particular kinds of atonal music, primarily the chanting of plainsong in church or on religious recordings. When she has her first attack, she is in church, waiting for her mother to finish with choir rehearsal, and her immediate interpretation of the epileptic fit is that she has received a vision from God.

Until this moment, religion has served to keep Murmur Lee from her mother, and so at first she is extremely worried that perhaps Jesus "loved [her] more than he loved Mother" (75), and that her mother will be furious. She attempts to keep the knowledge to herself until she is forced, because of the physical nature of the fits, to tell her mother. Because she has internalized the connection between her mother and religion, it is not surprising that, when she finally does admit to the fits, she describes them to her mother as "talking to God" (82). Instead of solidifying the wall between Murmur Lee and her mother, this confession effectively bridges the distance between them, and Murmur Lee accepts the place of religion in both of their lives. Narrating the story from an undescribed afterlife, Murmur Lee tells readers that, at the moment of confession, she had heard God's voice telling her, "'You can do it . . . make her love you'" (83). For young Murmur Lee, the epileptic attacks are her opportunity to regain what she sees as a lost connection to her mother. As long as the visions continue, she knows she will be the center of her mother's world, loved and cared for, even if her father remains absent.

If we continue to draw upon Lacan's theory of the symbolic father, we also see how Murmur Lee's supposed supernatural connection to the world of her mother's religion allows Murmur Lee to have, for the first time, what she sees as a normal family. Religion, as a father, is even given a human representative in the form of the priest, Father Jaeger who, along with her mother, introduces Murmur Lee to the world as a saint. As is the role of the father in the Oedipal family drama, religion stands as obstruction to the desire of the child, blocking her from her mother, until finally the child accepts the law of the father and begins to desire not the mother, but a mother substitute. In this case, the mother substitute just happens to be the father. Murmur Lee, at the tender age of five, develops a crush on the new priest, Father Parisi, who comes to witness her having a vision. Murmur Lee's reaction to this new priest is wrought with both familial and erotic tensions, and she feels pressed to explain that "Children have crushes, you know. This idea that we don't become sexual beings until puberty is hogwash. And I, in my rubber panties and sweet ruffles, took one look at Father Parisi and fell head over heels. I wanted him. And I wanted him bad, with all the passion that children possess but usually successfully hide from adults" (98). Despite the sense of taboo that usually accompanies any reference to the sexual lives of young girls, Connie May Fowler insists readers understand that Murmur

Lee's attraction to Father Parisi is more than a familial or religious one. In fact, Murmur Lee imagines that, because of her specialness in God's eyes, the priest will be allowed to marry her when she grows up and that he will be the father of "a houseful of sweet babies" (99).

When Father Parisi figures out that the child is suffering from epilepsy, however, he unintentionally reinstates the barrier between her and her mother, because he takes away her "special" religious status, showing the world that what seems to be saintliness is actually a disease. In revealing the truth, however, Father Parisi awakens in Murmur Lee a desire for reconnection to the mother, in the form of a "hunger for God" that Murmur Lee says "would stay with me up until my teen years, when it was supplanted by my appetite for sex" (101). The direct correlation between her desires for God and her desires for sex suggests that, in the case of Murmur Lee, religion and sex are both connected to the desire for caretaking—especially significant given that, as a teenager, she falls for and eventually marries an older, authoritarian man who, even her best friend agrees, seems to take the place of the parents who were, at best, absent from Murmur Lee's life following her brief stint as a "saint" (110).

Amongst Fowler's works, the mother trapped behind the barrier of her own problems is not a character limited to only *The Problem With Murmur Lee*. In reference to her own life, Fowler has spoken a great deal about the troubling demons her mother had to deal with and the ways in which those problems affected her ability to be a good mother. As a result, Fowler, much like the character in her autobiographical *Before Women Had Wings*, grew up believing that Jesus was a boyfriend who could keep her safe. While imagining Jesus as an emotional and/or erotic partner is not unusual for the subjects of this study, this particular eroticization appears to be a way of rebelling not only against society and/or southern etiquette, but also against religion itself, as reflected in the opposition between the imagined Jesus and the real abusive mother.

Bird, early in the novel, develops a love for Jesus, believing that Jesus will be there to protect her and love her. In fact, Jesus represents what she wishes she had in parents—caretaking and gentle dispositions. She believes that, if her mother were only "Jesus-like, all forgiving, and gentle to little animals," her father would be happy, and the family would be a strong one (10). Unfortunately, her mother is violent and vengeful, holding Bird and her sister Phoebe responsible for the failure of her marriage and family. She stands both textually and metaphorically in opposition to Jesus, and it is Jesus against whom Bird rails when, "after enduring a beating, I'd stomp into the bedroom and stare at that Woolworth picture of Jesus and . . . ask 'Why have you forsaken me?'" (50). Ultimately, though, despite being placed in opposition to Jesus, Bird's mother is not set against the Christian religion itself. Instead, she grows to represent what Bird sees as an Old Testament form of Christianity. After Bird has decided that she must read the Bible from cover to cover in order to be saved, she watches her mother stand up for her in a fight she has with a neighbor boy, and considers how her mother's actions fit her new religious worldview:

> . . . Forgiveness was too complicated. That's what was good about a wrathful God: simplicity. You were good or evil. Cursed or blessed.
>
> I looked at Mama. She was spinning the ashtray, lost in thought. We'd had a breakthrough. In the face of accusation, she had stuck by me, even lied for me. But then a chill clamped down on my bones as I realized what was wrong with a wrathful God. He could change His mind at whim, justifying His swift, crafty moves with rules He made up as He went along, rules that changed without warning. . . . I drew a picture of God. I bore down hard, nearly ripped the paper. A circle, a planet, dark and dense. Yes, a black hole. Not a speck of light. Sucks you in. Never lets you out. (226–27)

Because of her past relationship with her mother, Bird is unable to associate the gentle, kind Jesus with the role that her mother plays. She begins the novel wishing her mother were the caregiver that she sees in Jesus, but ultimately she sees her only as a cruel God who can simply change His/Her mind "at whim." Further, her mother represents a cage, or a trap into which everything good (the light) is sucked, and out of which it is impossible to escape. If the combination of Jesus and sex have previously given her a space of safety, this is the space that stands in opposition to that one. This is the space where nothing is safe.

This moment of dark enclosure and deification has a counterpart in Fowler's own nonfiction autobiography. In *When Katie Wakes: A Memoir,* the story of her life with an abusive lover who often reminds Fowler of her mother, she depicts her lover as a violent, humiliating deity who seems also to exist as an inescapable black hole: "Next it's down the hatch with your drink. The cigarettes and bar matches disappear into a pocket. You are huge. You are no longer an old man. You are God. Very Old Testament" (2340–42). Like her mother, her lover literally sucks things in—cigarettes, matches, a drink, and especially her. This scene comes directly after a moment when her lover had seemed kind, had seemed to be praising her in front of her coworker, and then had pulled the rug out from under her, insulting her and calling her stupid and ugly. Like her mother, he is seemingly random with his praise and his punishment. The parental divinity, her God/Mother, becomes her God/Lover as she grows older, but Jesus remains the same for her. He is the gentle, long-haired caretaker that both Fowler and her character Bird imagine as a child. Historically, when the Christian divinity has been "feminized," it is almost always Jesus who is feminized and not God. That it is her mother (or any mother, for that matter) who is re-imagined as the vengeful God of the Old Testament is thus both unusual and insightful. It points out that the disjunction between God and Jesus is not due just to Jesus' role as caretaker, but to often random acts of violence. Because her mother is violent, she is more like God than the sacrificial Jesus, and because she is violent she is, in essence, masculinized whereas Jesus, who is gentle, is feminized, resulting in a metaphorically bisexual interest in the Christ figure that will appear again in Fowler's adult love-life when her abusive lover will become her old Testament God while her eventual husband, whom she meets while living with her lover, reminds her of Jesus because of his "big brown eyes" (2349–55).

The idea of a feminized divinity (as opposed to the already-feminized images of Mary and the female saints) is not a new one to art and literature. Art historian Caroline Walker Bynum, in *Fragmentation and Redemption,* traces much of the late medieval art and literature that depicts a Christ figure whose penetrated, bleeding body is "female . . . lactating and giving birth" (82). Multiple paintings, for example, reveal Jesus feeding others from the wounds of his body—wounds which, as Bynum points out, are spatially represented as breasts. The feminization of the Christ, she writes, comes about in part because he, like women, feeds others both literally and spiritually. There is, of course, an analogue to this in the Christian sacrament of communion, wherein the believer either metaphorically or literally (depending upon the denomination in question) eats and drinks the body of Jesus during religious services. Her strongest argument, however, is her belief that the Christ figure is not human-like, as Leo Steinberg argues, because of his physicality or his genitality, but because he suffers—something that all humans, male or female, do.[1] Margaret Ripley Wolfe's point that women in the South "have adjusted themselves to the prescribed feminine roles of service and sacrifice" thus creates a bridge between Christ and women. Bird ultimately makes this connection herself when she realizes that the softly spoken, long-haired Jesus is not going to help her and, in fact, cannot help her at all. Instead, he is only able to offer her a shrug and the question, "Ain't love mean" (50). Jesus, Bird realizes, may be able to save her spiritually, but he, like the southern women who surround her, will not be able to help her from real, physical suffering (particularly because they themselves are suffering).

Bird, however, is not the only one of our characters who finds interest in a feminized Jesus figure. Rosemary Daniell struggles after her teen years between believing in/loving feminized and masculinized religious figures, and that struggle is directly reflected in her sexual choices. Most of Rosemary Daniell's works, including her autobiographies, unknowingly reflect the suggestions being proffered by feminist theologians Rosemary Ruether and Carol Christ, who are ready to dismiss Christianity as a site of empowerment for women, but readily admit to the power of some of its basic traditional tenets such as faith, prayer, and communion. Finding in Christianity, and in Catholicism in particular, a rich field of symbols, Daniell turns to religious imagery over and again in her depictions not only of southern women, but of female sexuality in general. Daniell initially turns to religion as a way to forget sexuality, as her culture demands. With the unconscious eroticization of Christ, however, she nevertheless retains a central fantasized male body. As she matures, this focus on Christ as a male erotic partner shifts, and Daniell begins to see Christ as a feminized figure who sacrifices himself to pain and suffering the way she believes southern women have always done. As the image of Christ becomes more feminized for Daniell, and she sees Christ more and more as a woman, she becomes more drawn to women as potential sexual partners. Eventually, Daniell seems torn between a masculine Christ-figure and a feminine, motherly one, resulting in an androgynous vision of the divinity.

The merging of the sexual into the spiritual is not unidirectional, however, and Daniell often depicts mortal figures, both male and female, as godlike. In fact, she outright refers to her erotic partners as her "gods" (*Flowers* 163) and posits that she has always been in search of a "god-man" (103). The reasons for this search, as Daniell casts them, arise from the ways in which she was brought up in small, highly religious, rural towns in the South. She was raised in a number of these small towns, with their requisite Methodist and Baptist churches, throughout Georgia, and her conclusions that patriarchy and tradition, including religious tradition, are the causes of her search for a god are supported by scholarship generated by a number of anthropologists and cultural critics who have studied such towns, including Anne Firor Scott, Valerie Fennell, Jean Friedman, and Shirley Abbott, and especially their understandings that within Christianity women must "inhabit the sphere to which God had appointed them" (Hill, *Solid South* 94).

Daniell sees and characterizes her mother as a victim of just such a system, leaving her ambivalent and concerned about the role of mothers and wives in the South. In *Fatal Flowers*, Daniell explains that her maternal grandmother had a great influence on the author's mother, Melissa Connell, and that the latter did whatever she felt she could to please her mother because of strict teachings that girls should honor and obey their mothers. Daniell explained in an interview, "I don't think I ever remember her [Melissa Connell] thinking for herself or thinking a thought that was different from the way she was brought up. That's what killed her finally, I think." And yet, despite Daniell's conviction that her mother never thought differently "from the way she was brought up," there is evidence that Connell must have struggled at least somewhat against what she had been taught because she was also a writer of sorts. Although she tore up everything she wrote because it was considered unladylike to write, she nevertheless wrote, indicating a desire, however small or subconscious, to break free of what she was taught. In the end, however, she continued to embrace the idea—perhaps because she wanted to believe in the ideals set before her by her own mother—that she would find a husband who would take care of her and provide for her if she just believed and worked hard enough, and behaved like a "good" southern girl should.

Daniell, in turn, was forced to struggle not only with these ideals, but also with the problems they caused in her mother's life. Daniell explained in our interview that, because her father was an alcoholic who would often fight violently with her mother, she felt a "stigma" attached to her life. If Daniell felt shamed because of her parents, then Connell, who was forced to deal directly with both the stigma of being a failed belle and that of having an alcoholic husband, likely would have felt doubly so. Daniell explains in *Fatal Flowers* that her mother was considered unsuccessful by societal standards because of her "alcoholic first husband" and "her years of unexpected struggle to support herself and her daughters." She adds that southern culture teaches "the degree of a [husband's] support was the measure of [a woman's] goodness" (7). In our interview, Daniell explained that she knew her mother had failed to find that support: "I saw what my mother had to do for marriage—she had not made a good marriage. She had to get on a bus and go downtown and work as a secretary." In short, for Daniell's mother, work shamefully marked that she did not have a husband who could or would support her.

Seeing the results of a family torn apart by these southern ideals, Daniell fought them, but in an attempt to please her parents, she also largely continued to teach these same ideals to her own children early in their lives, and even felt guilty when she failed to live up to the standards set by her mother. During her first marriage, for instance, Daniell would stay home with her children, reading "articles in *Ladies Home Journal* about how to be a better wife," and wake up early every Sunday and "walk down the dirt road to the Baptist church" (*Flowers* 145) with her kids while her husband slept. Even though she was questioning religion by this point in her life, she nevertheless felt it important to maintain a religious commitment to be a better southern woman and wife and to pass those ideals on to children. Furthermore, Daniell, like many southern women before her, felt that, by retaining a religious commitment and suffering for the sake of her abusive husband, she would be "good again, held in the arms of Jesus, as [she] had been at eleven" (145).

Eventually, however, Daniell's need to distance herself from her parents and their problems lead her to actively reject the traditional southern mores about religious and feminine roles. She began indulging in sex with multiple partners, experimenting with same-sex relationships, attempting to find answers through alternative, non-religious sciences (psychoanalysis, reality therapy, etc.), picking up men, having affairs behind her husband's back, and engaging in "unladylike" behaviors such as writing. Although Daniell has remarried and settled into a more conventional lifestyle, her need to distance herself from her mother still seems to require that she place her mother in direct contrast to herself. Such distance, however, seems to find a bridge in Daniell's fascination with the image of Christ's mother, Mary.[2]

Although Daniell herself was never Catholic, she places great significance on Catholic imagery and on the imagery of Mary in particular. This is unsurprising given Mary's representation as the most important mother figure in the Christian religion, even outside of Catholicism. Further, Mary has long represented for most people a kind of selfless humility that is expected of women, especially mothers. In his analysis of sexuality within the framework of Catholicism, Thomas C. Fox explains how the Vatican, in 1991, asked U.S. bishops to focus in their teachings on the "'Marian dimension' of the church" that "included 'the aspect of servanthood, lowliness and humility, which is emphasized in the life of Mary'" (239–40). For southern women, for whom wifehood and motherhood have long been a mark of success, Mary thus represents an unattainable goal of perfect self-sacrifice.

Daniell sees Mary as perhaps the ultimate suffering woman, or even the ultimate southern woman. In an exchange of email regarding Catholic imagery and the importance of suffering in Christianity, Daniell writes: "I find the imagery and the icons of Catholicism compelling and meaningful. To me they simply carry the images of Mary, the Crucifix, several steps further than the Protestant denominations. Also, a woman—Mary—is at the center. . . . It probably has to do with an identification with suffering—women's suffering especially—and the fact that suffering is a part of her life." That Mary is a mother is obviously relevant to Daniell, and that she suffers—the way her own mother did—is also important. However, Mary is also, as we see in her poem "Mary, Mary," an erotic figure, and her suffering is at least partially erotic in nature. The poem overtly deals with Christ's mother, but is obviously metaphorically also about southern women and potentially all women in western culture:

> Mary was a sucker—
> done in by the culture—

her role? to get screwed by God—
fall before His ghostly cock

then hang around the house
while the menfolks do their thing—
as carpenters, gurus—

her last scene?
a tableau: suffering over Him.
It goes on forever. (1–10)

While the culture referred to in the poem is ostensibly biblical, as
seen through the eyes of Daniell, the poem is obviously about southern woman in general, and specifically, perhaps, her own mother, to
whom she has also connected suffering. Christ's mother, like all "good
southern women," plays her role properly—just as her mother did. Mary
serves as God's sexual partner and then gives up the rest of her life to
her "menfolks," as Melissa Connell gave up her own dreams of writing
for the sake of her husband and her cultural demands. Mary's existence
is one of servitude, and her place in society is determined by her role in
Christ's life, just as a southern woman's role and status is determined by
her husband and children. In fact, after Christ's crucifixion ("her last
scene"), in which Mary is seen weeping at the feet of her son, "suffering over Him," she disappears from biblical text. Like the postbellum
mythologized southern woman, she is raised to a pedestal, but because
her son is dead, her role is fulfilled, and she becomes invisible as anything other than a statue. Daniell is also insistent, however, upon the
sexual aspects not only of the Virgin Mother, but of the divinity as well.
The "Virgin Mother" is depicted as a sexualized being who falls before
God's "ghostly cock." Daniell's choice to emphasize the sexual helps to
undercut the idea that Christianity is a sacred institution fully removed
from the corporeal realm.

Although the novel is not specifically about Christianity, Sheri Reynolds's *Bitterroot Landing* touches upon some of the same concerns as
Daniell's, especially in regard to the place of the Virgin Mary in understanding both the body and the spirit. Jael, the late-teens protagonist, has
spent her life in foster families. First she is with a hoodoo woman who

rents her out to male customers and whom she eventually and acciden-
tally kills. Then she is placed with the deacon of a local church who lives
in an isolated camp on the river and who eventually begins raping her.
Jael uses the sexual interest of a passing stranger to escape from River
Bill's house, and when the stranger, Thompie, leaves her stranded in a
forest clearing, Jael refuses to go back, learning to live in the wild. After
time has passed, though, Jael gets sick and is forced to seek shelter with
campers that she sees. The social worker Helen, who is assigned to her
case, places her at a live-in housekeeping job at a small Catholic church,
and Jael finds herself listening in on women's incest survivor groups
through a hole in the wall of her small room, leading to the beginning of
a recovery that will require both sexual and spiritual healing.

While working at the church (a place that already makes her nervous
due to River Bill's religion), she takes on the job of cleaning the statues
in the various shrines around the building, and finds herself growing
more and more fascinated with the statue of the Virgin Mary. While the
images of Jesus do nothing for her, she is drawn again and again to Mary
who, she explains, was "the first woman that I loved" (80). As well, she
pretends that Mary is her mother and then saves the water she uses to
bathe the statue, taking it back to her room where she "drank that water
like nectar" (81). Having never had a positive mother figure in her life,
she can only imagine that Mary is the perfect mother, the one who will
get her through any kind of trauma. She is not attracted by the other
religious figures in their shrines, and in fact dislikes some of the male
statues, but she comes to Mary any time she feels alone or confused.

When she asks Mary about the priest, Arthur, the Virgin tells her that,
while "Arthur means well," he cannot help her because "he doesn't know
much about physical love-making." By now, Jael has begun to traipse
slowly into the realm of the sexual in her own life, finding a boyfriend
whom she is trying to trust, but Mary's words still surprise her, especially
when she explains: "what the church forgets to teach you is that you
can't minister to the spirit alone. Don't neglect the body, Jael. Minister
to the body as well" (122). In the imagined words of Jael's Virgin Mary,
she finds the words that she subconsciously knows are true. They are the
words that she believes a good mother would tell her daughter, and they
involve the healthy combining of the spiritual and the sexual. Mary certainly doesn't privilege one over the other because, after Jael starts having

sex, she also reminds Jael not to "forget to minister to the spirit," since "You can't choose one or the other. You have to find a balance" (158).

It is this same balance that Chopin and O'Connor insist upon and that Daniell seems to be seeking when she imagines her own Mary as both an erotic and a spiritual being. Daniell's Mary, however, is unable to overcome the patriarchal rule of Christianity, and is stuck in a "tableau" of suffering that will continue forever. Jael's Mary has a lot in common with the "dark woman" statue that Jael herself makes out of clay and who instructs her that all women and all gods are part of the same being. The dark woman, similar to ideas of the sacred mother goddess, teaches Jael that she, like Ninah in *Rapture of Canaan,* ought to create art, and that the art should come from her very body, pushing her to paint using her menstrual blood. These paintings are certainly similar in scope to Ninah's rugs made with barbed wire, blood, and other elements culled from her daily life. In the end, Jael realizes that the dark mother and the Virgin Mary are teaching her the same lessons, and she has a dream of herself nailed to a cross with Mary and the dark lady nailed to crosses on either side of her. Each of these mothers represents a part of her, and in the end, she must be able to pull these parts of her together in order to heal.

Both Reynolds and Daniell, like the Franciscan priest Richard Rohr (quoted in Fox), see that to separate the body's sexuality from spirituality is a "disastrous theology" for a religion that is based on the idea that "God became flesh" (251). The compartmentalization of sex as sinful and religion as good eventually creates a need to combine the body and the soul, or physicality and the spirit, as a necessary step towards both a healthy religious understanding and a healthy sexuality. This need is also perhaps why Daniell's poetry is filled with women who wish for ecstatic marriages with Christ that will fulfill them both spiritually *and* sexually, women who suffer in hopes of redemption for imagined sins, and women who kill themselves rather than attempt to forge out a life that contradicts southern tradition. These are also women for whom even an ecstatic mortal relationship may allow for transcendence above the body and above bodily existence.

What Daniell will realize over time, though, is that the masculine figure of God with his "ghostly cock" becomes less traditionally masculine in the figure of Jesus. Christ as a mortal man is inevitably depicted as penetrated, the way Daniell believes all southern women are eventually literally and figuratively penetrated. She says in *Fatal Flowers*, "to be feminine, I was beginning to believe, was to be penetrated, blood-stained, bloody forever" (76). Furthermore, Daniell begins to believe that men are not the only extensions of Christ; through images of blood and sacrifice, women are also linked to Christ, and their status as savior is reified. Caroline Walker Bynum has done significant work in showing the ways in which medieval paintings and woodcuttings depict Christ as both male and female, uniting the two genders through sacrifices of blood and food from the body.[3] Her work shows how, even without her realization, Daniell's growing understanding of Christ as feminine has precedence.

This understanding begins, for Daniell, with the coming of her first menstrual cycle. While she has previously seen, in the image of Jesus, a potent male sexuality that attracts her, she begins to connect herself to him when she gets her period because of the religious teachings regarding the blood of Christ. If Christ bleeds, and she does too, it means she also has some power inherent in blood. She explains, "I sensed a new asset . . . just as in my favorite hymn, there was 'power in the blood,' and the blood meant we were women at last" (105). She says she "loved the red that swirled in the toilet bowl, or lay close to [her] body, warmly trapped in cotton" (105). Because both Christ and women are associated with images of blood, she can see herself as compatible with him and with male power. She begins to see in herself an "embedded penis" (12) that is the sign of male power for her. This sign of masculinity is complicated, however, by her belief that "to be feminine . . . was to be penetrated . . . bloody forever." What results, then, are images of herself and Christ as androgynous beings who are "part woman, part man—each of us wounded and bleeding" (103).

While through blood and suffering, an older Daniell can relate more closely with Christ and think of him as more than just an erotic partner, as a young woman she can never completely suppress the idea that Christ is linked to men and thus to sex. She writes, "It will be years before I begin to see the Christ as androgynous, like myself. . . . [F]or decades I will believe, like Mother and my grandmothers and their grandmothers, that my salvation lies first in a male God and then in a god-man—even a no good one" (*Flowers* 103). The "decades" Daniell speaks of give her ample time to question and change iconographic systems. It also gives her time to question this search for a "god-man" and the perfect southern marriage. During our interview, Daniell referred to the idea of marriage "as a form of restraint—almost like becoming a nun." She believes that this vision of marriage "would have been tied into [her] mind, at the time, with the image of Jesus because He was such a large part of the role of goodness." It is telling then, that Daniell begins to question marriage at the same time she begins to question her religion: "I started keeping a journal when Darcy was a baby, and started examining all the beliefs with which I'd been brought up, mainly my fundamentalist Bible Belt religious beliefs. I found myself questioning these things. Did I really believe in the Virgin Birth? Did I really believe Jesus was the son of God? And marriage—I started questioning monogamous marriages." Just as she starts to doubt monogamous marriages, she begins to wonder about "monogamous" forms of Christianity. She begins to wonder about her Protestant upbringing and to incorporate the iconography of Catholicism into her works.

It is through this embrace of Catholic imagery and a reconceptualization of Christ as an androgynous figure that Daniell does eventually choose to see Christ as more than just the ultimately masculine male. In fact, she makes what appears to be a self-conscious choice to see him as feminine, and in a chapter of *Fatal Flowers* aptly labeled "A Kiss for Christ my Sister," Daniell describes how she went from embracing a divine masculine power to a divine—and incestuous—female one. This change is chronicled in her poem "Liturgy," in which she repeats a stanza, changing the pronouns from masculine to feminine:

> For us   He allowed
> Himself   to be bruised
> crushedthe nails
> to enter His flesh . . . (26–29)

and

> for us   She allows
> Herself   to be bruised
> crushedthe nails
> To enter Her flesh. . . . (61–64)

Interestingly, the verb tense shifts from past to present—an indication of the continuation of a long history of actions on the part of women.

The switch from the masculine pronouns *He, Himself,* and *His* used to denote Christ to the feminine *She, Herself,* and *Her* to denote a female deity comes at the end of the poem, after a long description of a woman's visit to a gynecologist's office where she is "opened like / a purse knitted / unknitted vacuumed / & scraped hooked / like a fish" (45–49). Eventually the woman is penetrated with a "needle / in the perineum" (58–59). The act of penetration solidifies the synthesis of the feminine and the divine. Like Mary, the woman in the poem is a vessel, able to be opened and closed, her insides able to be scraped out, and her perineum able to be pierced. Her body, an object, is "scraped hooked," with the hooks imagistically alluding to the nails in Jesus' flesh and the thorns on his head. And when the procedure (perhaps a health procedure, perhaps an abortion—Daniell is purposely vague here, perhaps hinting that all such procedures are, in the end, painful and invasive) is done, "each time methio- / late is poured / into Her wounds" (65–67). Methiolate, a solution used for cleaning wounds, is often called "Monkey Blood" because of its staining blood-like color. That the woman can leave the gynecologist's office penetrated and stained with blood brings to mind images of the Christ, penetrated and bloody.

Within "Liturgy," the female speaker recognizes this similarity between women and Jesus and the resulting feminization of Christ:

> & standing behind
> the pews   I knew
> what every woman
> there knew . . .
> that it's not the up-
> raised arms   beard
> biceps: the power
> to push us into
> stirrups over bath-
> tubs under thumbs
> we worship but what
> lies beneath Her
> stained-glass skirts:
> cuntovaries   womb:
> the swollen secret lips   the soft pink

tits of Jesus our
hermaphrodite   our
Sister on the Cross. (73–76, 84–98)

Daniell not only recognizes the femininity of Christ, but gives him female genitalia and even argues that it is not the masculinity of Christ
that women worship or that draws them closer to Christ, but rather his
feminized nature. Interestingly, the images Daniell chooses to highlight
are the often sexualized ones; it is the reproductive organs, the "cunt"
and the "soft pink tits," that she foregrounds. In short, Christ becomes a
sexualized (perhaps brutally so) female figure. And yet this image is not
without license from within traditional Christian iconography, which
potentially allows for this feminization. The physical depiction of his
body, while highly eroticized, is often one of an androgynous, gentle man
with long hair. Even within Protestant iconography, he is often pictured
praying, a feminine, supplicant activity, and the sacrifice of his body for
the good of his followers obviously places him into the realm of the feminine, particularly for southerners.

In her *Gospel Hymns and Social Religion*, Sandra Sizer writes that images of Jesus in Protestant hymns are of a beautiful, gentle man who is
"not only loving and kind, but also charming and beautiful; He enfolds
the poor sinner in his arms, and to be in his presence is heavenly bliss"
(35). In another, commonly sung hymn, Samuel Stennett's "Majestic
Sweetness Sits Enthron'd," believers are told that Christ is the most
"fair" of all beings and is "sweet" and "radiant." Such a Christ is not the
hypermasculine southern man, described by Fennell and Ownby, who is
supposed to turn away from Christian ideals and spend his time having
sex, fighting, and drinking. Instead this is a man who, in every respect
except his ostensible sex, resembles a good Christian southern woman.

A change of interest from the masculine divine to the feminine begins for Daniell shortly after her mother's suicide. Daniell explains, "[T]
o free my repressed feelings of love and longing for my dead mother
had required, for me, an emotional and literal bisexuality" (*Flowers* 287).
Earlier in the text she remarks that, as a child, her love for her mother
had felt "shameful" (55) because of what she perceived as sexual abuse in
the form of forced enemas from her mother. Daniell now, however, turns
to women in search of that same love. After becoming involved with her

first female lover, she explains, "Aching for the mother I had thought I hated, I loved burying myself in her plush flesh, found solace in the salty sweetness" (224). She further articulates that she "had thought this beautiful woman would make a good substitute for mother" (224). What is perhaps most interesting is that Daniell begins to have "sexual fantasies in which [her lover] and [her] dead mother become one" (225). Daniell's search for a better, healthier relationship with her mother, a relationship she never had while her mother was alive, results in Daniell's developing sexual relationships with women who stand in as substitute mothers and also, perhaps, are able to help ease the guilt over what she saw as the "shameful" sexual feelings that the early forced enemas gave her.

In light of these feelings, and because of Daniell's tendency to eroticize religion and vice-versa, her search for a maternal figure through sex becomes particularly complex. While many scholars have posited that female same-sex desire is linked to or somehow contingent upon a search for maternal figures, Daniell's search is not just for a mother, but for a religious substitute as well. Thus, even though Daniell ultimately chooses a male as her life companion, her experimentations with women are fraught with both religious and incestuous connotations. Historic support for the idea of a "Mother Jesus" or a motherly Christian divinity comes as early as Saint Theresa, a medieval Catholic mystic with whom Daniell was familiar. Saint Theresa writes in *Way to Perfection:* "The soul is like an infant still at its mother's breast. . . . [I]t is the Lord's pleasure that, without exercising its thought, the soul should realize that it is in His company, and should merely drink the milk which His Majesty puts into its mouth and enjoy its sweetness" (73). Saint Theresa often describes Christ as a bridegroom with whom she shares ecstatic unions, but here he is a metaphorical mother who feeds the soul through his/her nurturing milk. While many hymns, including W. Hay and M. H. Aitken's Baptist hymn "We Leave it All for Jesus"[4] overtly create a Jesus who is both father and spouse, it is Saint Theresa who offers a mother who is also spouse. For Daniell, fascinated as she is by Catholicism and the early Catholic saints, such a combination may have offered a nurturing and healthy, though admittedly still incestuous, substitute for the eroticized patriarchal divinity of her childhood.

Daniell, of course, is not the only one of this book's subjects to develop an early correlation between parents and religion. For Daniell, the teachings of religion are tied deeply to the teachings of southern etiquette that her mother insisted she learn, and for some of Lee Smith's characters, the nexus of religion, family, and sexuality is even more problematic and intense. In her first novel, *The Last Day the Dogbushes Bloomed,* for example, the young narrator is so disconnected from her family that not only does she give them names that imply her isolation from them (her mother is the "Queen," her sister "The Princess," while she is simply Susan), she is unable to turn to them after she is raped by a neighbor boy. In other novels such as *Family Linen, Oral History,* and *Fair and Tender Ladies,* plots center on the themes of individual and family identity and the ways in which the two often collide. What all of her novels have in common, however, is that females, young and old, struggle to find a place where conflicting ideals can meet safely, whether those ideals are related to the sexual and the sacred, or passivity and action, or nature and religion. It is in the space of collision and/or resolution of these differing ideas that identity is either formed or lost (or, in some cases, both). In Smith's early novel *Black Mountain Breakdown,* Crystal Spangler is the epitome of Smith's early heroines who suffer the most from the inability to resolve conflicting ideas relating to family, sexuality, and spirituality.

In a moment eerily reminiscent of Bird's decision that her abusive mother is like a cruel, random God whose acts of kindness are never to be completely trusted, Crystal reminisces on the great "Ghost King" Clarence B. Oliver. Crystal is the daughter of a fading southern "belle" who, according to Minrose Gwin, "takes what comes and doesn't ask hard questions" (429) and a man who is slowly dying and has ensconced himself in his wife's front parlor where he reads Gothic poetry and terrifying stories to his daughter and her friend Agnes on a regular basis. Crystal, who is her mother's hope for a happy southern ending (she will win beauty pageants, she will get married, she will frost her hair, she will have children), is easily seduced by these terrifying stories and poems and would rather spend time with her father than do almost anything else, including playing with her friends or going out with her mother. Clarence B. Oliver fits into these Gothic stories easily. He is, according to Crystal, the "greatest of all" the ghosts who rule the days of the week. The ghosts, she believes, are color coded, with the black ones being the worst, and they come on specified nights, but Oliver is "behind all the ghosts, beyond and above them." This ghost, an analogue to God, is "as big as the world. He can do anything he wants to. He can kill anybody he wants to, anytime. If you . . . are obedient and fair with the colored ghosts, then Clarence B. Oliver will be there when you need him to help you out. But you don't mess around with Clarence B. Oliver. You don't ask him for anything unless you really want it so bad you will die if you don't get it" (36).

Like Bird, Crystal is aware of some all-powerful being whose control over humans seems occasionally random and always at least slightly untrustworthy. Like a genie with his own interpretations of wishes, Oliver is a ghost who shouldn't be called unless the situation is absolutely dire. Oliver is also a divinity who can and will, if the mood strikes him right, be there to help and protect her. Crystal's creation of Oliver seems at first to be a way for her to connect, through a Gothic invention, to the father who is so distant and isolated from his family, and so weak as to be non-viable as a caretaker. Although Oliver has never shown himself (Crystal is rational enough to know that physical ghosts aren't real), he provides more as a *potential* father than her biological father does in the way of protection. Oliver, who is definitely a God figure, is thus also a father figure. It is after all Oliver to whom she cries out when she is being raped by her mentally disabled Uncle Devere. She finds herself wondering, "hasn't she been a good girl?" and then, when Clarence B. Oliver won't answer her, she realizes that "Clarence B. Oliver fails, of course. She should have known he would" (230). Oliver, like her real father, is ineffectual when it comes to protection. In fact, shortly after the rape (the next morning), Crystal discovers that her father has died, leaving her with only her mother, from whom she has always felt distant.

In her essay "Nonfelicitous Space and Survivor Discourse," Minrose Gwin discusses Crystal's relationship with Grant, and makes a compelling argument for why the relationship between Crystal and her father must be seen as at least touched by eroticism, and her argument brings to the foreground that Crystal may in fact be trapped in the Gothic death-urges of her father and that Oliver ultimately represents the only way (through death) that she may find familial or erotic fulfillment. Grant, Gwin argues, seductively reads stories and poems to Crystal that leave her both "horrified and titillated"; he "demands Crystal's presence in the parlor more and more often," and when he "calls 'honey?' it isn't clear whether he is calling his wife . . . or his daughter" (426). Confining himself in one room of the house and demanding his daughter's presence therein is, in many ways, similar to the ways in which Fowler's lover and Bird's mother both work like a black hole, sucking in everything, especially those who rely on them. While it is true that Grant is dying, he neither acknowledges this truth nor attempts to overcome it to provide Crystal with any kind of caretaking. Instead, he more closely resembles the spider from the story he tells Crystal of "the spider and the fly"; the one who invites the fly in to its death.

Crystal's terror at hearing the story is understandable because on some level she recognizes that she *is* the fly in Grant's parlor. Gwin also argues that Devere is, at least visually, representative of Grant himself. She writes, "In conflating the seductive father with his 'retarded' rapist brother who 'looks so much like [her father] that it sometimes makes Crystal cry to see him' . . . *Black Mountain Breakdown*, both masks and unmasks the father's power" (425). The power, in this case, is the power to keep Crystal trapped in the space of the father, or what Gwin calls "fatherspace" (428) either by demanding her presence, seducing her into it, or even, in the case of Devere, forcing her through violence to repress knowledge of herself and the world around her, keeping her locked in that moment, even if she is unable to consciously remember it. In this light, Clarence B. Oliver seems the conflation of Devere and Grant into one being who is ultimately unable to save her. This seems to be why Crystal, even after hearing the voice of "God" (who she initially assumes to be Oliver) at camp, is unable to remember the repressed rape and eventually succumbs to its paralyzing capability.

Before Crystal gives in to that paralysis, however, she attempts to find ways around it. It is her inability to resolve her own conflicting desires and beliefs that make it hard for her to succeed. When she turns to religion, hoping to find security through salvation, there is the definite sense that what she is seeking is a return of the intense, scary gothic with which her father had once surrounded her. Her friend Jubal Thatcher promises her that religion will bring peace and quiet, but quietly is not how she first experiences religion. Instead, she feels a burst of intense emotion in a revival tent that leads to her conversion, making her feel "lost in all those flames." Furthermore, in the very moment of "giving herself to Jesus Christ," she feels as if she herself is "nothing at all" (128).

The loss of ego at this moment is a loss of identity, caused by an extreme outpouring of emotion, but unlike Jubal, she is unable to fill that empty space with newfound religion. Instead, four days after the revival tent comes down, after the frightening intensity has passed, she gives up on religion altogether. What she wants in her brief foray into religion is not the peace and quiet of spirituality, but a deafening, emotional cataclysm that will drown out the voices that speak to her of her rape. She will make a similar attempt when she runs away with a lover who is, like her father, artistic and, also like her father, depressed. When she finds his body after he hangs himself, there is no question that Crystal has been unsuccessful at overcoming the effect and seduction of her father's Gothic impulses.

Throughout many of her novels, Lee Smith continues the tradition of creating, in fathers and husbands, representatives of the divine who ultimately fail. The most glaring of these instances, however, occurs in *Saving Grace*. Grace, the protagonist, learns very early in her life to associate Jesus with her father. Virgil is the most important and significant member of her family and the church to which they belong. As the leader of the Holiness community in which they live, Virgil Shepherd is, much like Ninah's grandfather in *The Rapture of Canaan*, the arbiter of rules, regulations, and spiritual guidance for his family and congregation. It is hardly surprising that, to Grace, he begins to represent Jesus both visually and metaphorically. A description of him as he watches Grace play with her siblings is particularly telling: "And there stood Daddy, black against the sun. His white shirt and his white hair appeared to be shooting off rays of light behind his dark form . . . the whole time we played, I knew that Daddy was watching over us" (10). This image corresponds to much religious iconography and art that pictures Jesus and/or God with rays of light shooting out from behind them while they look down upon the world (and, of course, Virgil was at the top of a hill watching his children drink in and lay around the water in the spring below them—a perhaps intentional visual reference to baptism).

The conflation of her father with the Christian deity is further complicated by the way that he makes Grace feel. She explains that "[w]hen ever Daddy walked in the door, everything suddenly got real exciting. All the familiar sights and objects of our lives . . . took on a deeper, richer hue" (14). He is the kind of man who draws people "like bugs to a flame," and Grace "loved [her] daddy so much [she] could hardly stand it" (28). The love she feels for him is the kind of passionate love ascribed to lovers, and she uses the same kind of language to describe her feelings about her father that she will later use to describe her first lover. When her father speaks at church, his soft voice calls out to her, amongst the others in his congregation, in "that voice which would not take no for an answer," calling "Come back, come back to Jesus" (19) as if he were a lover seducing his beloved back into his arms. In ways similar to the hymns of Daniell's Baptist and Methodist churches, Virgil's voice and his presence draw listeners into an intimate relationship both with God and with the preacher himself (literally in many cases, as he has fathered five children by three mothers). However, his excessive sexuality and his neglect of his family make him a poor father and a troubling Christ figure.

During her early childhood, Grace learns to hate Jesus because of what she perceives as his influence over her family. That they have to constantly move, live with strangers, and never have a home of their own is blamed on Jesus. The real problem, of course, is not with Jesus, but with her father who is "so busy following the plan of God that he didn't pay [his family] much mind in general" (12). Jesus becomes the focus of Grace's misplaced anger. Because she feels that the family is not taken care of, Grace cannot see Jesus as a provider—just as she cannot see her father as one. Ironically, the caretaker and provider in Grace's family is the one figure that young Grace is most eager to isolate from her visions of Jesus. Her mother, who always "had all the time in the world" (4) for her children, provides Grace with both inspiration and a possible alternative to the Jesus who is Virgil's heavenly analog.

For feminist theologians who want to see a woman-centric religion, Lee Smith appears on the surface to offer such a thing. Critic Jacqueline Doyle argues that, by the end of *Saving Grace*, Smith "leaves us at the verge of the inexpressible, a radically revised Christian spirituality that is open-ended, indeterminate, mysterious and woman-centered" (275) and Rebecca Smith believes that Grace (and other of Smith's characters) "can move beyond the constraints imposed by a patriarchal society and a patriarchal religion . . . because God speaks to them in a feminine voice" (11). Paula Eckard and Linda Byrd also both see a sacred maternal emerging from the works of Lee Smith, offering an alternative to what Eckard calls the "patriarchal spiritual realms" (187). Because Grace struggles against her father and his religion and eventually is drawn to handling hot coals and going to church only after having a vision of her mother, Eckard believes that, "brought to the Father through the maternal, Grace is restored to a purer self" (189). This view of Grace and her mother, however, does not account for her mother's suicide, or Smith's own admission that Grace is, at the end of the novel, going off to the same church that Smith herself cannot imagine attending because of "the loss of identity" involved in embracing intense mystical holiness and because, perhaps more tellingly, such churches "put down women" and "put down or stamp out things [she believes] are basically good" (50).

Such churches tend to attract those of lower socioeconomic status, and are primarily located in country settings, away from cities and large suburban areas. Certainly in the works of Smith, but also in many other works, these churches are depicted as primarily patriarchal, where men occupy positions of leadership and women are relegated to support. But these churches also provide, as seen by anthropologist Patsy Sims who, during a week of visiting and interviewing various members of a snake-handling Holiness church, discovered that: "For a people who had experienced the harshness of life," the church, while being the ultimate arbiter of rules, was also the central social outlet and a place where people had the opportunity to at least metaphorically overcome the suffering and pain of their impoverished lives (130). Paula Eckard also points out that, for women, such churches and their services are a response to their surroundings, providing a "safety valve" for the frustrations of poverty and squalor. They provide "a promise of holiness in the face of poverty and misery" (179). The question Smith seems to be struggling with is what the cost is for the women who embrace these churches and the temporary refuge they provide. Her answer, of course, is "loss of identity," and if this is the case, then readers are forced to reconcile Grace's relationships with her mother and father with her decisions to return to the Holiness church. The reconciliation is a tenuous one based on ultimate feminine acceptance of a Christian, patriarchal divine, but for Grace, such reconciliation at least allows her to embrace both of her parents as instruments of the divine and to find a way to overcome (or at least begin to overcome) the separation of the body and the spirit, or the sexual and the sacred, in ways that Crystal Spangler never manages.

Even if Grace's ultimate decision to return to the church is problematic, it is a decision to act, as opposed to an inability to do so, and so Grace is likely one of the most successful of all of Smith's girls at finding a successful merging of the sexual and the sacred.

Before this merging happens, however, Grace sees Jesus as standing in opposition to her mother, so that anytime Fannie indulges in Christian ritual, it upsets her daughter. For instance, when Fannie takes up coals, even though it is something that Grace herself will later do, Grace cries and bangs her head on the floor out of frustration because she believes that Jesus is burning her mother (25–26). Even this moment of hatred for Jesus, however, seems misplaced since it is actually Grace's father who, in what is almost a literal enactment of the Oedipal drama, physically blocks Grace's path, keeping her from her mother's side. In her youth, of course, Grace is unable to see that Fannie's suffering connects her to the feminized Jesus figure. Eager to distance herself and her mother from Jesus, and too young to completely understand what she is seeing, Grace doesn't recognize that Fannie is one of the many female characters in Lee Smith's novels who fall into the category of the self-sacrificing southern women "burdened by responsibility and guilt" who "live out hard lives taking care of others, often subjugating their own needs, desires and ambitions in the process" (Eckard 4).

Unfortunately, Grace's unwillingness to see her mother as connected to either Jesus or other women is only exacerbated by the fact that even Fannie assists in building up the image of her father's association with God, making sure that Grace understands that her father "is a saint . . . a precious saint of God" (13). As well, Virgil is often away from home, creating a very definitive "family" space of which he is only occasionally a part (although he rules this family space as undeniably as Grant ruled Lorene's front parlor). Generally, Virgil is associated with churches, the revival tents, and traveling, while Fannie is always depicted as surrounded by children, in the home, or in nature. Grace's desire to distance motherhood (and in particular her mother) from the role of Jesus is complicated however by teachings that all things separate from Jesus are evil. The confusion she feels as a result is partly illuminated by an analogy she uses to help make sense of her guilt regarding her hatred for Jesus. When she feels that she might be possessed by the devil, she thinks he might be inside of her "growing like a baby . . . until I got so big that everyone could see, and everyone would know my awful secret" (4). The metaphor, combining the devil and evil with motherhood and children seems to equate pregnancy with sin, and consequently women, including her mother, as the bearer of sin.

What Grace is able to see only in hindsight, however, is that, despite Fannie's association with motherhood, she is never really able to move beyond the childlike love she feels for her husband to become an actual caretaker for her children. Looking back, Grace admits this lack of "motherliness" and suggests that "it was not that Mama couldn't do these things—it was just that she was so caught up in Daddy's ministry" (23). Fannie thus unintentionally forsakes her children for Virgil because, in many ways, Virgil is more than just her husband—he is also her savior and deity. He is the one who saved her from a life of sin, the one who took care of her, and the one who, in a very real sense, rules over her. She allows herself to become a child to him, and thus is unable to fully be a mother to her own children. And it is this relationship that Grace unknowingly mimics, following in her mother's footsteps. Furthermore, it is a relationship she will continue to repeat as she grows older, involving herself over and again with men who remind her of Jesus and her father while falling into the patterns of submission and childishness set by her mother.

Complicating her relationship with her father and Jesus even further is the never discussed but inescapably incestuous nature of Grace's feelings. As she begins to awaken sexually, she is attracted to a substitute father figure who not only looks like her father, but is related to him. Her half-brother, Lamar Shepherd, "*looked* like Daddy" (70) and when he walks into a room she's in, her reactions are similar to the ones she has to her father: "It was like all my senses had been tuned up—colors were brighter, sounds were louder, and everything seemed so important" (77). Her feelings for Virgil and Lamar cause Grace to see the world in heightened awareness and ultimately with new depths of sexual and religious understanding. Lamar, much like her father, will become, during her relationship with him, associated with Christianity and with Jesus and become like a new deity for Grace.

That Lamar inspires a religious fervor in her is clear when Grace thinks of the church camp weekend and how she will have to be a "grown up girl" there with Lamar, and it is only after she has intercourse with him at the church camp that she speaks in tongues and gains, momentarily, the gift of prophecy. He inspires in her the same feelings that Jesus inspires in the others at camp, and she feels about Lamar the same way she had felt during the church services. The heightened emotions that the she and the other congregants hear while listening to her father preach about Jesus are the same emotions that fill Grace when she has sex, and for both the congregants and Grace, the result is an ecstatic expression of faith. It's hard not to be reminded here of de Beauvoir's commentary that, rather than simply borrowing "erotic vocabulary" for moments of ecstasy, women who feel either physical or mystical ecstatic love react the same because they have "only one body at [their] disposal" (673). De Beauvoir's thoughts on the woman in love who is so like a mystic in her behaviors and feelings reminds us that, ultimately, Grace and other women cannot escape the very real physicality of the body, and the body is always involved in the emotions as well. Grace takes this idea to its logical conclusion and reacts to Lamar by prophesying and speaking in tongues—she has a moment of ecstatic vision brought about by sexual ecstasy that she achieves with Lamar.

Of course, Lamar originally becomes a substitute for her father not because of his religious connections, but because of the way she feels that he "was trying to take care of [her]" (82). Because neither Jesus nor her father has taken care of or protected her or her family, Grace looks to Lamar to fill that caretaker role, but Lamar, like Virgil, will ultimately be a poor caretaker. As he becomes more like Virgil, leading in the Holiness community, handling snakes and preaching to the congregation, he becomes more like him in Grace's mind as well, and, as if to finalize the connection between Virgil and Lamar, Lamar becomes deeply associated with libidinal excess. Though he will remain for only a short time, it is enough time for him to seduce both Fannie and Grace, which will lead to Fannie's suicide and Grace's desire to disavow herself of sexuality altogether. She understands, without being able to voice it, that her mother has died because her mother could not deal with own sexual desires or the guilt she feels for having them. Rather than attempting to move beyond her mother's guilt, the young Grace takes on her mother's identity *and* her mother's guilt, traveling with her father, helping him preach to other congregations, and compartmentalizing her sexuality in an attempt to completely forget about it.

The desire to escape carnality will eventually lead her to marry Travis Word, another preacher in another Holiness Christian community. Literally "the Word" as opposed to the body, Travis represents salvation for Grace, and she understands that she "worshipped him" for his "faith, and his strength" (168). Although she does not see it, her relationship and eventual marriage to Travis are as much a result of feelings regarding sexuality and spirituality as her relationship with Lamar. While Lamar reminded her completely of her father—including in his libidinal desires—Travis represents spirit without the body, the opposite of her father. Unlike her father, Travis controls himself and his emotions, but he ultimately provides a tragic and telling example of what happens when the body is disconnected from spirituality. While she finds out that Travis had "a special weakness" for "pleasures of the flesh" (168), he is so adamant about the flesh being sinful that, after they *do* have sex (on rare occasions), he will "fling himself down on his knees, praying in anguish to be cleansed" (197). For the first time, Grace is able to have sex without the associated guilt of premarital prohibitions, only to find herself faced with the guilt associated with the body's "natural" impurities. Even this guilt, however, is at first acceptable, if it means she can escape from her father's raw sexuality.

Travis, instead of providing Grace with a husband and partner, seems to replace her father as an authority figure. Thirty years her senior, Travis calls her the little-girl name "Missy" and forbids her doing any work. Her only job is to get pregnant and then spend her time playing with her child as if the child were a playmate rather than a son. In many ways, then, Grace has become her mother, relying on her husband as if he were her father. Just as Fannie's only role was to keep her children company and play games with them, Grace is kept away from the hardships of life. And, just as Virgil insisted that his infidelities were Fannie's cross to bear, Travis attempts to convince Grace that the sinfulness of sex is hers. Eventually, though, it will become apparent that Grace cannot simply escape her bodily desires, and she will fall in love with Randy Newhouse, a man who, even more than her father, represents raw sexual appeal and with whom she runs away, moving from an all-out denial of the body to an all-encompassing embrace of the most squalid, sexual things she can imagine.

If Travis represents the word without the body, then Randy represents the body without the word, and once Grace is no longer the pretty, sweet girl, tempted by his seductions, he loses interest in her and begins an affair with another, younger, woman. His response when confronted by Grace is one that comes practically written from a book on southern male stereotypes: "You ought to know what men are like, their nature, I mean. It's normal. But you're not normal. You never were normal. It's all black-and-white with you" (241). Randy places the blame for the destruction of their marriage on Grace for not understanding how the South works. Because she wants stability and a faithful relationship, she is not "normal." Randy's pronouncements are not entirely inaccurate, however. He is wrong because Grace, despite her upbringing that runs slightly in contrast to the southern norms, performs the duties of a southern wife almost down to the letter. She attempts, early in the relationship, to convince him of the power of God, she makes him feel that her charms are all for him, and she lets him think that it's only the power of his masculinity that drags her down from her pedestal for brief periods of time.

Yet, for Grace, everything is "black-and-white." She has spent her life attempting to compartmentalize her spirituality away from her sexuality, and such separation has left her fractured, confused, and reliant upon others to tell her what is wrong and right. She has certainly rebelled from her father's church, but her rebellion does not mean she does not still believe that his doctrines were correct. Still believing in his, as we have seen, hypocritical rules and regulations, she has no choice but to hate herself for backsliding, and this self-hatred comes out in her choice of men who she knows will ultimately punish her the way she feels she deserves. There is a definite similarity between the way Grace feels in her various erotic relationships and the way that Connie May Fowler's work suggests that abused daughters feel. The guilt, the self-recrimination, and the involvement with other abusive partners mimic the childhood experience. Grace, despite believing that she has traveled far from her father and his church, has never actually left it, and it is this psychic space that she must confront before she will be able to integrate both aspects of her life into a normative space. She is still, as Randy declares, "not normal."

Eventually, Grace is led back to both the physical and psychic spaces of her early childhood through a series of events that resemble a Christian conversion narrative. As her father has taught her, Grace knows that everyone has a conversion story. His involves seeing serpents and hearing the voice of God. Such a conversion story is similar to those heard by Patsy Sims during her interviews with the Holiness Church of God in Jesus Name, wherein men meet God in the woods, hear the sounds of rattling serpents, and are violently struck dumb with sudden, sometimes frightening, revelations of truth. Grace's story, however, is decidedly less violent, though no less sudden or frightening. It is also significantly more feminine in nature, as is made clear by the pattern that her conversion follows. While searching for Randy in order to bring him home, she goes into a bar and picks up two men, taking them back to a hotel room for sex. Reaching the traditional "low point," she wakes up feeling "the worst I have ever felt in my whole life, both spiritually and physically. I went in the bathroom and threw up" (245). What Grace is throwing up here is not just the meal or the alcohol from the night before, but every meal and every drop of alcohol from her whole life—she is throwing up her past, purging herself of everything to make way for something new. As many scholars of mysticism have noted, the first step towards a true mystical encounter is the emptying of ego that holds individuals grounded to their mortal life. Since, for most people, conversion is the closest experience an individual will ever feel to mysticism, it makes sense that conversions also generally have a sense of emptying, sickness, or even near-death that precedes the actual moment of conversion.

Now emptied, Grace stops briefly at Uncle Slidell's Diner, a Christian restaurant, and hears a baby crying. She wanders out onto the attached "Love Tour" golf course in the snow in an attempt to find the crying child. Traveling the length of the course, a course containing mock-ups and scenes from the Bible, starting at hole one with the story of Adam and Eve and working her way towards the nativity scene and the birth of Jesus, she finally comes upon the baby in the manger and realizes that it is time to change her life. Paula Eckard explains that, in this moment when Grace is chasing down the crying baby, "Smith inverts [the] image of Jesus as the idealized lover into a pitiful crying infant who guides a shaken Grace towards home and, ultimately, to salvation" (186). The Jesus represented by her father and her various lovers has been replaced by a Jesus who cries out for a mother, inviting Grace to enter into Christianity not through the door reserved for "backslid" women, but through the door reserved for the sacred mother.

In order to fulfill that role, though, Grace will need to come to grips with her relationship with her own mother, and to do that, she needs to return to the space of both her happiest and saddest memories of her mother, the psychic and material space where her ideas of motherhood were most thoroughly formed, the house at Scrabble Creek where her mother died. It is on this journey home that she feels for the first time as if she is being born again: "I felt suddenly, completely *alive* in a new way, a way that made me realize I had only been walking through my life" (253). This new life, originating with the sound of a baby, drives her to visit her infant son's grave, where she sees, from a distance, Travis Word and has a vision of his life as nothing but "days of duty" stretching onwards until Travis finally kills himself (263). Whether or not Grace truly has a premonition of the end of Travis's life or not, the point is clear—Travis's life is incomplete and long, dreary and deadening. Travis has not committed suicide, but he may as well have. While she knows that she "had left a good man . . . for a bad one," she also knows that she cannot go back to Travis (263).

Before she finally returns to the house at Scrabble Creek, she also visits former friends, who let her know that her father has died of a snake-bite. It also seems that community opinion about Virgil has changed; no longer is he seen as the saint he was when she was younger; instead, his former congregants see him as a "blot on God's church" (256). Like the men that Grace is gaining the courage to leave behind, her father has finally and completely failed, betrayed by the very beliefs he had held. Now that Grace knows for certain that neither her father, Randy, nor Travis represents a viable option for her future, it is no wonder that she is "seized by wonder and fear" when an old congregant, Doyle Stacy, tells her that she needs to come back to her father's old church because, even without her father, it *is* in fact "the same old church" and "the same old God" (266). Doyle's invitation brings one last bout of anger from Grace, who contemplates how she has been "living a lie with Travis" and then "worshipping flesh and the things of the world with Randy" (267). On the surface, she is furious with Doyle for harassing her to go to church, but her anger is, for one last time, the misplaced anger from so long ago. Her father taught her that Jesus and grace were the only ways to get to heaven—that actions did not matter, and that forgiveness was paramount.

But, much like Lee Smith herself, Grace has long seen these explanations as excuses for disgraceful actions. Like Bird in *Before Women Had Wings*, Grace sees that forgiveness is too complicated. Her anger at those who believe in this method of salvation is truly an anger at the way such a belief has been used to perpetuate and excuse the very sins that the church preaches against. Travis tells her the opposite, that actions are important and that good deeds and intentions are as important as forgiveness in order to achieve salvation, but his ideal good deeds exclude her sexuality, demanding of her an impossible separation of body from spirit. Because she subconsciously knows this, she moves as far away from Travis as possible, ignoring the spiritual side of her life completely for many years as she lives with Randy. Eventually, though, when she has run as far as she can from her upbringing, she is forced to return in order to move at all. At this point, she has the choice to fall into the paralysis of Crystal Spangler or to find a new way to look holistically at her life.

The story of this running and the journey back is Grace's testimonial. Throughout the novel, she retells the testimonials of others, including her father's conversion story, her mother's story of the night she met Virgil, even of Travis's time in the war when he succumbs to temptation in Japan, but each of these has fallen into the realm of patriarchal language and structure. There is always an unambiguous calling and a definite, tangible result (her father's hair turned white after he heard God, her mother took her children and left her sinful life behind her, Travis took up preaching), and the defining figure in each of these is the patriarchal Jesus who calls them to follow. Grace's testimony, however, is ambiguous and uncertain; we do not know the result of the events that occur in the moment of or after her conversion. As Jacqueline Doyle writes in "'These Dark Woods Yet Again': Rewriting Redemption in Lee Smith's *Saving Grace*," "Gracie's own 'testimony' is neither fixed in meaning nor well rehearsed" (276). While her testimony is certainly viewed through the lens of her adulthood, it is not the self-edited, half-fictional, mythological testimony of the people around her. Finally, the calling from Jesus comes to her not through a powerful male voice, but in the language of motherhood.

The message here is fairly clear—her demons are related to motherhood, and in particular her own mother and her fears that she is in fact her mother's daughter, subjected to her father's religion and her father's view of faith. Perhaps she, like her mother, is powerless against the guilt that Lee Smith sees as her "great disease" (Ketchin, 172) and possibly the great disease of all southern women. The more Grace has attempted to distance herself from her mother, the more she has actually become like her, tracing her steps backwards. The relationships her mother had of which Grace is aware are the inverse of her own; her mother started as a dancing girl, worshiping the flesh with a seedy man; then she married Virgil and gave herself to her husband's religion in a relationship that resembled that of an incestuous father and daughter rather than that of a married couple, finally ending her life after being physically seduced by Lamar. Grace, on the other hand, first experiences a relationship with Lamar, then marries Travis, allowing herself to become a pampered child, and finally ends up with a seedy man with whom she enjoys the pleasures of the flesh to the exclusion of all else, even procreation. However, just as we do not know the story of Fannie prior to the first relationship mentioned, we do not know what will happen to Grace now that she has left Randy. It doesn't seem coincidental, then, that it is at this juncture, after having created an inverted pattern of her mother's life, that she is called to a spiritual awakening by the voice of her mother in the house at Scrabble Creek.

The "rebirth" that she undergoes leaves her like a child, very much in need of a mother. Her sight, like that of a newborn, is weakened by the glare of the snow, and she comments more than once that she needs to "protect my eyes from all this light" (267). Like a newborn, she is naked, walking across the house to touch her mother's possessions and look out the windows (270). When she hears her mother's voice telling her, "it's time to come to Jesus" (269–70), she doesn't even hesitate to do what her mother tells her. She puts on her mother's clothing (taking on her identity once again, the way she has previously done by taking on her mother's guilt) and then, just as her mother has done in the past, she handles hot coals without getting burned. Considering all of the men in her life—Lamar, Randy, her father, and Travis—she lets go of each of them, listening instead to the words of her mother, and crying out to Jesus, "'I am coming now, I am really coming Jesus,'" in what Paula Eckard calls "an orgasmic reference that blends the spiritual and sexual into one" (188).

By the end of the novel, she is laughing as she gets in the car to drive off to church because "the spirit is a joyful thing" (272). She listens to the bells from the churches chiming and says it "feels like a wedding day" (272–73). For once, the wedding in question is not Grace's marriage to a man who will force her to shut off some part of herself, but a marriage of all of the aspects of her life—her sexuality, her spirituality, her love of nature, and her identities as mother, daughter, and lover. Marriage is a particularly apt analogy here because marriages (at least the kind that would be announced by the ringing of church bells) are spiritual events that bring people together in the eyes of God, but they are also invested with a feeling of the secular—everyone knows what happens on a wedding night. The excitement of the bride and groom is as much about the joining of two bodies as it is about the joining of two spirits—usually even more so. Grace has fought off the demons of her past that have kept her compartmentalizing bits of herself and her psyche, and is finally ready to pull them together to create a whole being. As she drives off to church, she even thinks about the angels that she and her sister used to make in the snow, as opposed to the demons she has had to fight,.

The problem now, of course, is that we don't know what happens next—Grace's testimony and her journey up to this point have shown us only that she has decided to leave the men behind and to leave behind the identities that they have attempted to impose upon her. She has taken steps to distance herself from patriarchal forms of religion and culture and embraced the feminine in the form of her mother, even taking her mother's clothes as her own. However, what complicates this embrace of the feminine is that her mother, the most significant role model for the feminine that Grace has, was never actually able to overcome the patriarchal forms of religion that caused her to kill herself out of guilt and shame. Grace has invested her sexuality in Lamar, who resembles her father, then in Travis who tries to deny the body, and then finally in Randy who exalts the body to the exclusion of the spirit, only to find that none of them has worked. She finally has to turn to the only other model that has incorporated spirituality and sexuality into one, and it is, at best, a flawed model because of her mother's suicide. If she follows in her mother's footsteps, will she then also end up committing suicide at some point? Although we have no answer to this question, and Lee Smith herself seems unable to imagine a way in which the Pentecostal Holiness faith can combine in a healthy way with sexuality, the ambiguousness and the uncertainty of the novel's ending leaves us with, if nothing else, hope that Grace's journey will take her to a place where, as Paula Eckard suggests, "without question, the body and voice of the mother and the religion of the father have brought the daughter to salvation, wholeness, and a full acceptance of self" (190). Such a statement seems premature in light of her mother's suicide, and our lack of knowing whether Grace accepts the guilt and fear that come along with her father's religion, but it is one that Smith certainly seems to want us to believe is possible.

Although Lee Smith, Rosemary Daniell, and Connie May Fowler all significantly deal with the role that mothers and fathers play in the developing place of sexual and spiritual growth in the lives and minds of their daughters, it is important to realize that, ultimately, all of these authors are concerned primarily with the growth of southern girls as they deal with the etiquette and expectations that culturally surround them and that family is the predominant creator of culture in their lives. Dorothy Allison, for example, returns time and again in her stories and essays to the role of family in the growing morality and identity of children. It is through parents that the rules concerning acceptable behavior are passed down, and through parents that girls learn the rules of patriarchal society, even when those rules have tragic results, as in not only the case of Bone, but in her own case as well. In her novel *Cavedweller,* she deals even more expressly with the relationship between mothers and daughters, and the character Cissy, removed from Los Angeles to the small town of Cayro, Georgia, finds that her sexual growth is hampered by the lack of a strong relationship with her mother. She finds the room and ability to grow and mature only after metaphorically entering a relationship with a "motherspace," in the form of cave exploration.

When she is in deep inside caves, obvious symbols for wombs, she finds that she is able to express her sexuality in ways that she cannot do in the light of day. Further, as Karen Gaffney writes, although "Cissy always felt uncomfortable in her own body . . . after several caving trips, she experiences a new sensation of feeling 'happy in her body'" (55). This idea of motherspace exists in seeming contrast to Gwin's "fatherspace," and offers an alternative place in which healthy development may occur. When Cissy considers that the dark of the cave feels "female" and that "God was dark" (276), she is making a connection between the obvious female, sexual imagery and God in such a way as to almost imitate some of the moments already discussed, primarily those in Smith's works. In the works of Sheri Reynolds, as well, relationships with parent figures are of primary importance to female protagonists. In *Bitterroot Landing,* Jael is shuffled from one abusive parent figure to another. First, her adoptive mother "rents" her out to men, and then she is adopted by a church deacon who eventually begins to have sex with her against her will. It is only after she escapes this father and puts her faith in both an imaginary non-Christian goddess mother figure and the Virgin Mary mother figure that she is able to find her way to safety and into a church-run incest survivor's group where she can begin the healing process. The combination in Reynolds's book of religion, sexual trauma, and parental incest means that this book fits in well with the others in this study, though it may seem, on the surface, a less obvious work to choose. Ultimately, it is in the works of Lee Smith, Rosemary Daniell, and Connie May Fowler that we see the most interesting and, at the same time, troubling ways in which the addition of parental and familial connection adds to the study of the heterotopic space of sex and the sacred in the South.

CHAPTER 4

Mysticism and Masochism or Religious Ecstasy
and Sadomasochistic Delight

Pain, whatever else philosophy or biomedical science can tell us about
it, is almost always the occasion for an encounter with meaning. It not
only invites interpretation: like an insult or an outrageous act, it seems
to *require* an explanation.
—DAVID B. MORRIS, *Culture of Pain*

For Christians, suffering is never meaningless.
—JOSEPH AMATO, *Victims and Values*

In his 1905 work *Three Essays on the Theory of Sexuality,* Sigmund Freud
made the (now primarily debunked) argument that, because masochism
is a naturally feminine state, women are naturally masochistic. This argument, of course, is based on the idea that masochism is a state of weak
passivity—a masochist is naturally submissive, and since submission and
weakness are normally associated with the feminine, females must, by
nature, be masochistic. Despite objections to this definition, it is hard, as
Jessica Benjamin argues, to ignore the underlying cultural assumptions
about femininity upon which this definition is built: "though we may
refuse [Freud's] definition, we are nevertheless obliged to confront the
painful fact that even today, femininity continues to be identified with
passivity, with being the object of someone else's desire, with having no
active desire of one's own" (87). In 1924, Freud wrote his most influential treatment of the subject, "The Economic Problem of Masochism,"
wherein he defines masochism as a repressive function and explains that

"moral masochism" is that masochism tied predominantly to guilt, similar in function to repression itself. These definitions problematize the study of masochism as anything other than pathological and, as a result, sociologists, psychiatrists, theorists, and even masochists themselves have had to wrestle with definitions that seem at times overly reductive and at other times too inclusive.

Most often, however, when faced with the masochist or with masochism, the most common response is silence. We find ourselves at a loss for words. In teaching Dorothy Allison's *Bastard Out of Carolina* to a group of college sophomores, for example, I could not get one student to begin a discussion over Bone's violent fantasies of punishment and fire. It was as if the scenes themselves did not exist, and when students were asked specifically about Bone's masochism, most of them initially refused to see it as more than a disturbing and pathological response to the abuse she suffered at her stepfather's hands. Allison herself, on the other hand, is an open practitioner of S/M for whom masochism holds an important, even vital, meaning to her life and sexuality. Her feelings on sadomasochism, and masochism in particular, differ from those of the students. They, like Freud, want to see masochism as repressive—a way of hiding the pain and anger. Allison's definitions, though they do not deny that there is sometimes a relationship between masochism and abuse, are more in line with Michel Foucault's. Foucault, unlike Freud, sees sadomasochism as potentially positive and productive of, at the very least, pleasure.[1] The titillation of black leather, fuzzy handcuffs, or "whips and chains" aside, however, most people still see masochism (or sadomasochism) as a perversity or as a result of some trauma.

When we take the sex out of equation, however, and look at pain by itself, everything changes. Within the realm of acceptable commodities such as sports and beauty, pain is often acceptable and even encouraged. After all, "chicks dig scars," and "beauty is pain." The very concept of pain is undeniably historically constructed. In his study *Victims and Values*, Joseph A. Amato points out that pain becomes completely infused with political meaning and is inseparable from identity politics: Who suffers? Who doesn't suffer? What value should be placed on their suffering? In his award-winning *Culture of Pain*, David B. Morris examines this historical construction of pain to show not only how people suffer, but how history has viewed pain and suffering both biomedically and spiritually. Examining the relationships between pain and beauty, pain and religion, pain and sex, and pain and medicine, he is able to show how, throughout history, pain as a concept has been interpreted and endowed with meaning.

The meaning of pain obviously depends not only on the sufferer, but on outside interpreters as well. Morris reminds us, for example, of the belief on the part of whites in the antebellum South that slaves did not feel pain the same way as white, "civilized" beings did (38–40). As a result, behavior, expectations, and consequences were molded by the "understanding" that slaves could work harder with less stress on the body, take more severe punishments, and survive with fewer of the basic needs of food, clothing, and shelter. Other examples include, of course, a long history of mystics, saints, and martyrs who have suffered for religious or spiritual reasons. The question, though, is what sexual pain, the pain fantasized by Bone, or indulged in by Allison herself, has in common with the religious pain suffered by religious worshipers such as Catherine of Siena or Teresa of Avila? Critic Francis Kunkel, in his analysis of several well-known works, decides that there is no more than "a linguistic similarity" (183) between religious and sexual imagery, and on the surface such an answer might well fit descriptions of sexual and religious suffering. Underneath the surface, however, it appears that the similarity runs deeper. As mentioned by de Beauvoir, the very fact that both divine love and mortal love must be filtered through the body may explain part of this similarity, and for the mystics and the masochists in the literature of southern women, both mysticism and masochism result from a desire for transcendence and/or communion, and both ultimately produce similar types of pleasure and/or psychologies.

An obvious place to start, then, is with the work of Dorothy Allison, particularly, but not exclusively, with her novel *Bastard Out of Carolina*. Although my sophomore students were loath to discuss the masochistic elements of Bone's life, many critics have dealt specifically with her fantasies. While many have come to the conclusion that Bone's masturbatory fantasies are indicative of a repressed sexuality, some, such as Ann Cvetkovich and Katherine Henninger, have come to believe the opposite—namely, that Bone's fantasies and daydreams give her the ability "to salvage some pleasure from pain, some power from powerlessness" (99) and that the sexual trauma suffered by Bone can be viewed as productive (as opposed to merely reductive or repressive) of sexuality and sexual identity (370–77). Henninger, in particular, sees Bone's fantasies as another form of narrative—a story that she can control—and that such narrative control allows her to gain mastery over some small part of her life. Henninger is correct in that such fantasies do allow Bone to create a safe space for the exploration of (physically) her body and (mentally) her sexuality. After meticulously cleaning a grappling hook and chain she has found in the river at her Aunt Raylene's, she locks the hook around her and masturbates: "It was mine. It was safe. Every link on that chain was magic in my hand. . . . I was locked away and safe. What I really was could not be touched. . . . Somewhere far away a child was screaming, but right then, it was not me" (193). The violent potential of the hook and chain are here transformed into the locking mechanism that can shut out the actual violence from her life and allow her to safely explore her body and her desires. In this moment, her masochism seems less a desire to hurt herself than a desire to reconfigure the very idea of pain itself.

Similarly, the humiliation that she feels at the hands of Daddy Glen is reinvented, through her masturbatory fantasies, into pride: "When he beat me, I screamed and kicked and cried like the baby I was. But sometimes when I was safe and alone, I would imagine the ones who watched. Someone had to watch—some girl I admired who barely knew I existed, some girl from church or down the street, or one of my cousins, or even somebody I had seen on television. . . . [I]n my imagination I was proud and defiant. I'd stare back at him with my teeth set, making no sound at all, no shameful scream, no begging. Those who watched me admired me and hated him" (112). Bone, by creating a space where she can subvert the objectifying gaze of others to her own pleasure, manages to find a safe outlet for sexuality that, while not denying her abuse, produces what will ultimately inform her sexual identity.

Critic Deborah Horvitz sees this sexual identity, however, as problematic. She argues that, because Bone is "unable to imagine anything but horror associated with sex or sexuality . . . Bone con-fuses—conflates as well as mistakes one for the other—sex with being a victim of violence" (44). I would argue, however, that the reinvention of the violence into pride and pleasure through fantasy lessens Bone's personal acceptance of and association with victimhood. Rather than mistaking violence for sex (which she certainly does at first), she uses sex and pleasure to rethink her relation to violence. Michael Uebel tells us that masochism "brilliantly carries out the work of defending the self from an engulfing fear of the entire universe by inviting one part of it to invade and ravish the subject" (394), while Tina Portillo, an S/M practitioner, writes that, instead of violence, she chooses "S/M as the vehicle for expressing the emotions that threaten to overwhelm" (50) and that during such play "the world makes sense to [her]. . . . S/M is a point of sanity that serves as a formidable buffer against the insanity . . . all around me on a daily basis" (50). Through her fantasies and the pleasurable masturbation that accompanies them, Bone does, as Gearheart indicates, invite one part of her life—the violence she suffers—into her life in order to mentally "ravish" her, but she is able to redirect her feelings of violence (both the violence done to her and her desire to commit violence) towards a productive end that does, as Portillo hints, give Bone a place of sanity wherein the violence and the abuse can be reinvented as a productive element as opposed to a repressive one. Bone's ultimate connection to her (presumed) lesbian Aunt Raylene is thus not merely a rejection of male/female relationships and the inherent violence that she has seen in them, as some critics have suggested, but is instead a continuing rejection of victimhood that allows her to still retain the pleasure of her fantasies.

Dorothy Allison, herself a victim of childhood sexual abuse, sees in her own life the potential for the transformative nature of violent fantasies and what Freud calls erotogenic masochism. In her essay "Her body, mine, and his," included in the S/M-positive collection *Leatherfolk*, she writes that S/M sex is more than sex for her: "it is the intimacy of [women's] bodies, the insides of them, what they are afraid I might see if I look too close. I look too close. I write it all down. I intend that things shall be different in my lifetime" (48). Through the acts of sexual intimacy that combine violence, pain, and dark fantasy, she foresees the creation of difference, or transcendence during her life. Like Bone, Allison also finds the acts of *looking* and *seeing* important. She will *look* at the women too closely, she will *see* what is inside of them and, ultimately, she will write it down into narrative.

For Bone, the acts of seeing are also necessary for translation into narrative, and narrative is necessary for translation into survival. When she is telling herself the dark fantasies of Daddy Glen's beatings, it is important to her that she be watched. Significantly, her fantasy watchers, rather than representing the traditionally objectifying male gaze, are female. Because they are female, she is able to refocus the objectification and turn her watchers into witnesses who can help her transcend her role as victim.[2] However, even if we accept that the gaze is still objectifying, as Horvitz says, this gaze "inverts the more usual configuration of scopophilia in which a male 'gaze' is directed toward a woman, as she imagines herself the enviable focus of the objectification" (17). Bone is thus, Horvitz seems to be saying, both objectified and, more powerfully, objectifier. This is also the role Allison takes with her female lovers in "Her body, mine and his." She is the watcher, the witness to things these other women try to hide, and the objectifying gaze that pins them down. She is also, however, the watcher who, through the very act of looking, is able to help transform herself and the women she is with. She becomes a witness to their most traumatic secrets, the same way the watchers in Bone's fantasy become witnesses to the abuse she suffers.[3]

Witnessing, in both *Bastard Out of Carolina* and in Allison's life, leads to written and oral narration, and eventually, in the case of Allison, to art. (One could make the argument, as well, that Bone's storytelling is an earlier form of this same literary art.) Suzanne Gearheart, in her study of Foucault's and Freud's understanding of masochism, explains this relationship succinctly when she says, "art, like sado-masochism, may involve the transformation of pain into pleasure" (16). Just as Foucault sees the potential of production in unequal power relations, Henninger and Cvetkovich see Bone's fantasy life as productive of identity. Gearheart points to the sadomasochistic nature of this viewpoint. Because "power implies the existence of inequality, subordination, humiliation, or pain," she believes that "it is primarily the concept of sado-masochism that can account for the conversion of such an experience of displeasure, whether it is inflicted on others or on the self, into a source of pleasure" (6), but it is not merely her violent fantasies of pain and humiliation that help Bone convert "displeasure" into pleasure. Bone looks to religion and, particularly, to gospel music as a potential artistic pathway between the anguish of her life and a place of security and pleasure. Just as she uses fantasy to mentally begin a transcendence beyond her abuse, she turns to religion in search of meaning. In this search, just as in her fantasies, she yearns to have someone witness her at her moment of transcendence, this time as she is being "saved": "I wanted the church to fill up with everyone I knew. I wanted the way I felt to mean something and for everything in my life to change because of it" (152). Reminiscent of both Bone's sexual fantasies and Allison's autobiographical essay, these desires call for pain to be transferred into pleasure through an act of witnessing that gives Bone's suffering meaning.

It is also, however, the very moment of transcendence, the liminal place that is neither saved nor lost, that Bone wants to occupy. In an earlier fantasy, she imagines herself tied up in a haystack, with fire about to burn her to death, and it is at the moment right before her rescue from the haystack that she orgasms (63). As well, she climaxes during a fantasy of being left to die while birds pecked at her—certainly not dead, but at the threshold of death. This same moment of in-between-ness occurs in her religious fantasies: "It was not actually baptism I wanted, or welcome to the congregation, or even the breathless concentration of the preacher. It was that moment of sitting on the line between salvation and damnation with the preacher and the old women pulling bodily at my poor darkened soul" (151). By having witnesses to this moment where she is *in the act* of transcending from one state to another, she is able to inscribe her life with meaning, and the meaning posits her as special, loved, and safe. It is the very place and moment of identity creation that she fantasizes. It is the same moment, one might argue, that David Morris describes, when discussing a painting of Saint Sebastian's martyrdom wherein he is staring upwards towards the sky while archers pierce him with arrows from below, as "suspended between the world of the body, which he has not yet entirely abandoned, and the world of the spirit, which he has not yet entirely attained." Morris sees such a moment as giving Sebastian "power to see a truth beyond the horizon of earth and matter" (127).

For Bone, who is, through pain and abuse, trapped in an agonized bodily existence, this moment in the church, or the fantasized moment in the haystack, provide her with potential transition into a truth—or a meaning, as she puts it—beyond that bodily existence. Bone is, in essence, a would-be mystic and martyr who has suffered and is seeking a meaning for that suffering. For Christian mystics, Morris argues, suffering "assumes specific meaning as a sign that points to a realm of eternal truth beyond the perishable body" (129), and the visionary pain that mystics have felt "regularly takes up a position that sets it in conflict with competing systems of power" (138). If we look at Bone's fantasies (both the religious ones and the sexual ones), we cannot deny their similarities to the "visionary pain" that Morris describes. Bone seeks escape from her bodily life and the systems of power that trap her body into the categories not only of white trash, but also of victim. She looks for escape into a mental or spiritual life that, because of age and inexperience, she is not completely able to fathom. She is able to imagine it only as a painful hunger for "something—Jesus or God or orange-blossom scent or dark chocolate terror" (151). While she is unable to imagine what that spiritual fulfillment might be, she does consider that it might be found in gospel music—the artistic or *narrative* form of religion, and this narrative form combines sexuality, bodily yearnings, and a quenching of spiritual thirst. Gospel music, she thinks, "was the real stuff. I could feel the whiskey edge, the grief, the holding on, the dark night terror and determination of real gospel" (169). It is interesting to note the use of the "dark night" description here—perhaps a reference to St. John of the Cross's "dark night of the soul" during which the soul yearns and aches for understanding of the divine in the same way that Bone yearns for meaning in her life.

The question of whether Bone's yearning and her fantasies are ultimately productive is answered in many ways by Allison's own autobiographical writing. While yearning without acquisition can certainly be devastating, particularly if the subject doesn't understand, the way that Bone doesn't, what she is yearning *for* or where the yearning comes from, the act of yearning itself, much like the act of becoming or transcending, can allow for the formation of desire and the incorporation of desire into identity. As an adult, Dorothy Allison, having suffered similar abuse as a child, writes that "Women lose their lives not knowing they can do something different" and that "even children go crazy, believing the shape of the life they must live is as small and mean and broken as they are told" (51). Bone's knowledge of the shape of her life is formed by watching her family, primarily her aunts and mother, and knowing what is permitted them, but also by watching the desire and violence apparent in the way they live.

Through telling their stories and by creating her own, Allison begins to be able to produce a narrative of her life that includes desire. As she begins to finally indulge in her lesbian desires, it takes her time to understand that the violence of her abuse has an effect on that desire. She writes, of the first woman she ever made love with, "I cried because she smelled like him, the memory of him, sweaty and urgent . . . breathing her in prompted in me both desire and hatred, and of the two feelings what I dared not think about was the desire. Sex with her became a part of throwing him off me, making peace with the violence of my own desire" (48). What is unusual here is not that sex with women helps her throw off the memory of her male abuser, but that the abuse itself becomes part of that desire—not in that she craves the abuse, but that she understands the way that her abuse mimics desire, and the way her own desire is "violent." Until now, desire and violence both have been associated with her abuse, and now she reinvents them, incorporating them into her own desires—understanding, for perhaps the first time, the ways in which her own yearning may be productively answered. Allison writes that she "knows" she is "supposed to be deeply broken, incapable of love or trust or passion," but in the end, her response is to say "I am not," and part of the reason why she is not a victim is because of "the nature of the stories I told myself to survive" (69). Ultimately, then, her fantasies, her yearning, and the narrative she creates for herself produce an identity that goes beyond a lesbian/straight dichotomy to incorporate all the "queer" identifications implied by her fantasies. As evinced by her own willingness to write about and engage in a sadomasochistic lifestyle, Allison has claimed violence and desire, turning them towards the purpose of pleasure and reenacting that pleasure over and over until the emotional and mental pain are unable to victimize her. Allison herself writes, "I am doing it as much as I can, as fast as I can. This holy act. . . . The holy act of sex, my sex, done in your name, done for the only, the best reason. Because we want it" (48).

Through her religious and sexual fantasies, Bone expresses a desire for the kind of transcendence that Claire, the young would-be martyr in Valerie Martin's *A Recent Martyr*, also envisions. Claire, the young Catholic novitiate, is, on the surface, both a mystic and a masochist. When asked by her would-be lover Pascal what the mortal reward is for her near-asceticism, her response is that it's religious ecstasy (63). What she seeks through her ritual prayers, and the ascetic practices of self-flagellation and occasional self-starvation, is a purging of the bodily desires that will leave her open to being filled by the divine in an ecstatic moment of union. Feminist scholar Sarah Bracke, in a study of the Catholic movement Comunione e Liberazione in Italy, points out that for Catholic saints, particularly female saints, "bodies are quite central (in terms of bodily transformations, torture, etc.), *but only to be transcended*" (emphasis mine, 30). It is this transcendence that Claire craves. When her confessor asks if she wants to be a saint, she is overwhelmed by emotion and cannot deny it (135).

Given the inevitable pain and gruesome endings of the saints before her, Claire's desire to be a saint certainly seems masochistic. As Morris points out, suffering and pain hold "an almost sanctified place in the process of sainthood as a test or trial of faith" (129), and certainly Claire knows this. In fact, her friend Emma, after Claire's death by stabbing, believes that Claire "knew that when she met her death . . . it would be the last test she must pass before she could have that union she most desired" (201). What makes Claire's understanding of this pain masochistic as opposed to simply tolerant, however, is that, instead of fearing or simply accepting the pain, Claire welcomes it, even attempting to relate to the suffering of Jesus through self-flagellation on those occasions where she feels bodily or mentally overwhelmed (one is reminded of Portillo's comments on the use of S/M play). However, an important question is whether self-inflicted pain brings Claire closer to the divine, or closer only to her own physical body. In describing the two possibilities for such pain, Morris explains that, while most pain "chains us down to the mortal world" and "keeps us centered in the flesh," visionary pain "contains the power to transcend the world and the flesh" and "employs the body in order to free us from the body" (135). Evelyn Underhill, in her well-known study *The Essentials of Mysticism*, argues that, on the other hand, many ascetic practices designed to encourage visionary pain are "almost certainly disguised indulgences of those very cravings which they are supposed to kill, but in fact merely repress" (23) and that many "visionary" experiences are in fact not true mystic experiences because "mystical consciousness is perpetually open to invasion from the lower centres" (30). If Claire's attempts at mystical pain are, in fact, not influenced by the "lower centres," then the numerous visions she has can be viewed primarily as visionary. However, Claire's need to constantly engage the body in order to escape her body (her self-flagellation, yes, but also her semi-starvation and need for constant physical activity and exercise to the point of exhaustion) draws repeated attention to the body itself, and it is possible to see her need for physical exhaustion or pain as sublimated bodily or sexual urgings.

In order to see whether Claire's self-inflicted pain and self-denial are "visionary" or "indulgences," it is useful to compare her to the novel's other primary female, Emma. Emma Miller is Freud's classic erotogenic masochist. She and her lover Pascal indulge regularly in the sadomasochistic play to which she introduced him. Emma is also Martin's homage to Emma Bovary of *Madame Bovary*, and like Flaubert's heroine, Emma feels that her life is almost completely devoid of meaning. Her husband fills her with "perfect numbness," and she sees for herself "a future of unrewarding jobs that stretched out meaninglessly" (20–21). She craves the intensity that her failing marriage and dull job are unable to give her; however, such intensity is seen, even in the more outgoing environs of New Orleans, as inappropriate.

For both Emma and Claire, raised and living in the southern city of New Orleans, there is a definite etiquette that is required by women, and Emma has been, heretofore, a successful practitioner of proper southern behavior. She has gotten married to a stable man with a good job, she has had a daughter, and her job is one that allows for her to work part-time so that she might spend more time with her family, but this life has left her bored and ultimately rebellious. Even Claire, who ought, perhaps, to understand how Emma feels, tells her to leave the more sexually and emotionally thrilling Pascal and go back to her stolid husband. When Emma suggests that maybe her husband is not a good one, Claire tells her that she should go back "even so" (183), yet it is just this overwhelming need to follow southern female etiquette that seems to drive Claire away from marriage and family life altogether and into the arms of the Catholic Church. Recalling the scene between Claire and her confessor, we are reminded of her absolute contempt at the thought of being a wife, a mother, or a working woman (135). She even tells Emma that, while her body can "easily take a beating," she has no desire to "subject either [her] soul or [her] body to the will of someone who values neither" (96). The implication is that "submitting" to marriage and motherhood would do exactly that—subject her to someone who values neither her body nor her soul. The view here of marriage (of any heterosexual sex, for that matter, since she is also loath to give up her virginity) could hardly be called positive. Emma may be successful by southern female standards, but she is miserable while Claire decides to throw all of it aside and ends up disconnected completely from humanity. Neither solution (compulsory heterosexual marriage or religious isolation) allows for a positive outcome, and Martin seems inclined to point out the problems inherent in both of them, problems that stem from the inability of either character to accept her culturally created role.

When Emma first meets Pascal, she's in a library reading that Gothic classic *The Monk* while Pascal is deeply entrenched (or so he would have the world believe) in seventeenth-century French poetry. As her reading matter might indicate, Emma (like Madame Bovary) has been influenced by romances and stories of passion. Emma, bored, lonely, and attracted to the emotional excess of the Gothic writers, is ripe for a seduction, and so Pascal, noting her choice of books, decides to seduce her. Almost immediately, they begin a sadomasochistically influenced relationship wherein Pascal dominates, hurts, and occasionally humiliates Emma for both of their pleasures. Quoting Havelock Ellis from his *Studies in the Psychology of Sex,* David Morris points out that "'Pain acts as a sexual stimulant because it is the most powerful of all methods for arousing emotion'" (208), and so it is hardly strange that Emma is attracted so strongly to pain and humiliation, or that she encourages Pascal to hurt her during their lovemaking and responds more passionately when he does. The book opens, in fact, with a scene of humiliation wherein Pascal pulls up Emma's skirt, exposing her nudity to a bus full of people, furthering the humiliation by sexually stimulating her in front of the bus driver. Rather than getting angry at Pascal, Emma gets carried away in the moment, ignoring the bus driver's disgust or her own embarrassment as she "forgot where [she] was" (4). And when the two of them return to Pascal's apartment, the humiliation she has suffered and the embarrassment she feels turn into a desire for both pain and pleasure: "I was sad and excited and so completely humiliated that I found myself hoping that he would hurt me" (5).

Afterward, Emma returns home via the streetcar, lost in what appears to be a peaceful trance, and as she rides the bus, she watches people, projecting her own feelings of calm and introversion onto everyone: "no one so much as returned [her] look. Each pondered, as [she] did, the secret self" (5). The release of emotion that she feels as a result of S/M creates both an inward connection to herself and an outward distance from others. She is contemplating not the world around her, but her inner "secret self," and her understanding of her fellow riders is relegated to assumptions that they are as self-focused as she is. It is only a few pages later when Claire, after being transported to a rapturous state by listening to religious music, has a similar moment: "She had been drawn into the music and then, mysteriously, lifted by it . . . until she lost all touch with it and could not have described, or even recognized again, what she heard. She listened instead, and not without wonder, to the insistent pulsing of her own heart" (8). Both women have, through a moment of ecstasy, become alienated from their fellow humans and are lost in thoughts of their own secret selves—the selves that are somehow inside and out of their bodies at the same time. Sarah Bracke offers a possible explanation for this ability to escape the body through the body when she explains that, "for all the emphasis on the body in Christianity, the point is the spirit that is 'in' the body, which may be called spirit mind, soul or God. It is this spirit or mind that is equated with solidity, with identity, while the body is considered something extremely volatile. The body then becomes something which the mind must expel in order to retain its integrity" (30).

Although Bracke's comments would seem to apply more strongly to Claire than to Emma, even Emma has a need to push beyond the body and to "escape" from it as if it were a cage. Readers learn that, even after Emma eventually gives up Pascal, she does not give up the desire for physical pain. In fact, she explains that she begins to inflict pain on herself (as Claire had done) to help provide "relief from frustration, particularly of a sexual nature." "Self-inflicted pain," she explains, "has a calming effect; it clears the head, diminishes one's fascination with the ego, and, most important, gives one the sense of having taken some real action against the everyday foolishness of the body" (94). It is this "everyday foolishness" which neither Emma nor Claire is ultimately able to stomach. For Claire, it leads to self-flagellation in her cell-like room, and for Emma it may start with her sadomasochistic relationship with Pascal, but it ends the same way—in self-inflicted pain that helps her escape the body. In this way, then, masochism looks a lot like mysticism, and sadomasochistic practices are certainly comparable to ascetic ones.

Emma's relationship with Pascal reflects Claire's relationship with the divine in more than just physical ways, however. Through the sadomasochistic nature of her sexual trysts with Pascal, Emma is able to recognize what she calls a longing for death, and it reminds her of "Claire's determination to have her spiritual Lover" (138). She feels, while having sex with him, that she is "ready to go beyond the limitations of [her] senses," but only if she can take Pascal with her. What she seeks here is not (as Pascal called religious ecstasy) "masturbation," but a joint experience with another. She wants to move beyond her body and her sensual experiences, but she wants those experiences to be shared with someone else. This is closer to Claire's desire for divine union than readers may grasp upon a first read. Emma explains that "there is something to be said for a lover with whom one can be united *only* in death" (138). It seems here that Emma's craving for death is not the longing for the self-annihilation that some critics have seen in her masochism, but a longing for the temporary loss of ego that comes with bodily transcendence.[4]

Emma certainly seems aware of the connection between her and Claire when, during her final meeting with Pascal, she finds herself thinking about Claire and Claire's quest for a mystical union: "I knew all at once . . . I had found the love that would put an end to me, created a bond that was stronger than my will, and I couldn't break it. What Claire said she wanted, I had: a lover who would consume me entirely" (167). Ultimately, what both women want with their mortal and/or divine partners is more than just escape from the physical body itself; what they seem to want *is* a kind of consummation that will leave them empty and devoid of ego in preparation for a perfect union. In Freudian terms, of course, the id is most closely associated with the body and with bodily hungers, including sexual desires, while the ego is aligned with the mind's interpretation and regulation of those desires. Freud posits that the masochistic urge is the superego's punishment of the ego, resulting in emotional and mental cravings for bodily hurt that ultimately pleasures the id's desire for sexual satisfaction. Martin's characters want to be released from such physical and bodily ties, and seem to rebel against any idea of a "superego" that reflects cultural imperatives. Instead, masochism for these characters is a break from such demands, including breaks in their ties to other humans, who may also represent those same cultural expectations. It is only when Martin's characters are isolated from others, if only in an imaginative state, that they are able to find meaning—or, more to the point, to escape from all meaning that is attached to the world. For Emma, this understanding comes to her only after Claire's death, when she realizes that "the great release of death . . . was not from bondage to our lovely planet . . . but from one another" (196). Like other saints and mystics, Emma and Claire both seem to realize that pain and anguish come from human connections and mortal love that keep them bodily and spiritually bound in chains to one another.

Martin seems to understand more poignantly than her characters, however, that the penalty for such disconnection from other mortals, either through divine union at the expense of human connections or through a masochistic separation of the soul from the body, must be death, either real or metaphorical, which comes as the final, culminating test before divine understanding. For Claire, this test comes in the form of two men who attack, rape, and eventually kill her as she is finishing the twenty-mile trek back to her convent after finally being given permission to leave the outside world and return to her preferred, cloistered life. Only moments from achieving what she has been waiting for, Claire is forced to sacrifice her virginity, what she has seen as "the best thing" about her (95), and then to sacrifice her life. This is, as Morris has pointed out, the final test for sainthood, and it is no coincidence that proceedings begin shortly thereafter for Claire's sanctification.

Claire's death scene is also reminiscent of the final time that Emma and Pascal meet, the moment that could well represent a metaphoric death for Emma, in a complete loss of ego. For both Emma and Claire there is a moment when each is being physically choked, and when the lack of breath makes them acutely aware of the bodily pain they are suffering: "The big man put his forearm across her neck, choking her cruelly. Her back was pressed against his stomach, her hands pinioned behind her. . . . [T]he pressure at her throat was intolerable; she could hear the sound of her own desperate spasmodic breathing everywhere in her head" (187). And ". . . there was a dreadful ringing in my ears, but most of all, deep inside, there was a dry, throbbing, agonizing pain that made me want to scream. . . . [H]e pressed his forearm across my throat with such force that I cried out. I could neither move nor breathe" (163).

That each of them is faced with death by choking is significant. The

loss of breath forces each into an internal moment where she is aware
not of divine union, mystical communion, or even sadomasochistic
pleasure, but only her own body. This is in direct conflict with the images of Saint Sebastian and Saint Teresa that Morris discusses. Instead
of transcending the pain, each woman is trapped within the pain, unable
to move beyond it. For Claire, the only thing that lies beyond it is death,
and if Claire is right about the union that comes next, Martin keeps it
from readers, showing them only her bodily death in a seemingly meaningless murder. But for Emma, there is something more beyond her test.
Emma, at the hands of Pascal, suffers not from S/M play but from a real
rape. She asks him multiple times to stop hurting her, and he simply
refuses to hear her, insisting afterwards, falsely, that she had said she was
okay to continue. This rape may look, on the surface, like the S/M play
that they have been engaged in all along, but it is different not only in
that she asks him to stop and he refuses, but also in the way that Emma
internalizes the moment. She does not "transcend" this moment; she is
unable to escape her own body to a place of ecstasy, and is aware only of
her own pain.

Normally, S/M play leaves Emma so calm that she "could not have
been ruffled by an explosion" (31), but after this meeting with Pascal,
it's all she can do to keep her calm long enough to walk out of the hotel
room. She does, however, walk out. And it is this walking out that most
clearly marks both the similarity and the difference between Emma and
Claire. If, in fact, what Claire has been engaging in through her ascetic
practices has been a form of mysticism, then it would make sense for her
final moments to be less focused on the body. However, if what she has
been engaging in all along has been a form of erotic and/or masochistic
desire and fulfillment, then it is logical that, in the end, like Emma, she
is more closely connected to her pain. This is not a moment where she,
like Saint Sebastian, is looking up into the heavens, her mind already
transcending her body. Further, unlike Emma, Claire is unable to survive
this final test, and one wonders if Evelyn Underhill's thoughts on most
"mystics" apply to Claire: "The innate longing of the self for more life,
more love, and every greater and fuller experience, attains a complete
realization in the lofty mystical state called union with God. But failing
this full achievement, the self is capable of offering itself many disguised
satisfactions; and among these disguised satisfactions we must reckon

at least the majority of 'divine favours' enjoyed by contemplatives of an emotional type" (30).

In light of both Underhill's considerations of mystics and Emma's final survival, Martin seems to want readers to understand that masochism as we think of it may ultimately be preferable to mysticism. The desire for divine union, the hunger for mystical experiences, and the unwillingness to completely connect to anyone on a mortal level leave Claire unprepared for life, and her death is the ultimate expression of that lack of preparation. By not allowing Claire her moment of divine, upwards-glancing, revelations (she is instead focused only on the knife, the bringer of her death), Martin makes us question whether Claire's mystical intentions were ever more than the attempt at escape with which her confessor and others accuse her. During her erotic S/M play, Emma is able to frequently escape the confines of her body and find a peaceful calm that makes her life more bearable, but by denying the bodily, erotic nature of her own self-inflicted pain, Claire is ultimately trapped in that very body. Emma, unlike Claire, is finally able to accept that she is connected to her body and to others. The time she has spent helping others, the time she has spent with her daughter, and even her friendship with Claire, all help to show her the bonds she has with others, while the shocking and very real, non-pleasurable pain of her rape show her the inescapable connection she has to her body. Unlike Claire, however, Emma is able to walk away from her attack and create for herself a meaningful life. It is her understanding of the physical/sexual nature of her masochism that allows her to differentiate between consensual and non-consensual pain, and to overcome the latter. For Claire, who never understands her own body, but only attempts to escape it, death can be the only real, final escape. Ultimately, as Foucault points out, consensual sadomasochism produces states of pleasure, states of calm, and a kind of peace that Emma, through her acceptance of both body and soul, achieves but that Claire, with her rejection of all things bodily, does not find.

Another possibility, of course, is that, despite her desire to lose her ego and transcend her body, Claire is unable to let go of her ego in the same way that pain allows Emma to do. Critic Chris White points out that "acts of humiliation in ordinary terms represent an annihilation of values and beliefs that underpin self-definition and self-protection" and asks where the "erotic thrill" is if "humiliation (play) deprives the submissive of an apparently safe and stable identity, and leaves him/her floundering, bereft, afraid, hovering on the brink of self-annihilation" (88). But, White says, such a reading of humiliation play requires that identity be a stable, fixed entity incapable of fluid change. Instead, he argues, many pieces of erotica dealing with sadomasochism "seem to inscribe something more fluid, that goes beyond or against safe identity as a slumbering inert thing, and into a domain where self as an experience is multiple, flexible" (88). While White's study is of 1890s erotica, such a statement might hold truth even for today's literature, particularly that of Martin. McClure, for instance, believes that "[a] literary text apparently invested in masochism may actually subvert the masochistic positioning of the female subject by refusing hermeneutic possession and exploiting masochistic pleasure—that is, pleasure in the loss of a stable identity" (2). Martin's various novels, definitely invested in masochism, provide a practical stable of characters who find themselves and their identities in a constant state of flux. Emma, through S/M play, is able to erase the culturally decided identities she has previously accepted, becoming someone new, or even becoming no one at all—a radical stance that allows for the blank space of potential and change.

We are reminded here of the ways in which both Judith Butler and Homi Bhabha argue for the fluidity of identity that is constantly being created and re-created. The space of Emma's S/M play is a space for Bhabha's "sites of collaboration and contestation." Claire, for her part, seems to fall into White's first category of believers—the believer of the static, fixed identity. As an example, we need only to look at her final letter to Father Paine, wherein she points out her own difficulty in letting go of her sense of self in order to embrace the divine: "there is indeed another reality, and . . . it is somewhat frightening because it requires the total surrender of my will and finally, ultimately, the wholesale destruction of my ego. This is hard. If I'm going into another world, I cry out, I want to be *me* in it" (181). Despite her intellectual understanding of what it means to be a saint, she is unable to give up her fixed sense of identity in order to follow through emotionally on that understanding, whereas Emma, in her ability to completely lose herself in a masochistic moment, is constantly reinventing her own identity in a fluid, non-fixed way. Emma, by the end of the novel, is capable of rewriting herself in new and constantly more holistic ways. As Martin herself points out, "Emma is in a masochistic relationship. But she leaves it of her own free will and feels pretty good about it" (Smith, "An Interview" 17). It seems to be the masochism itself that has helped her to "feel pretty good about it," especially considering that her indulgence in the sensation of pain does not stop when the relationship does.

Rene Girard, in *Deceit, Desire, & the Novel*, discusses Madame Bovary's brief bout with what he calls "pseudo-mysticism" after she is left by her first lover, and his discussion is interesting in light of not only *A Recent Martyr*, but also other of Martin's works such as *Set in Motion* and her short story "Surface Calm." Girard argues that Madame Bovary's desire for intensely passionate lovers and her desire for religious expression both stem from the same "deviation of the need for transcendency" (62), and he quotes Jules de Gaultier, who writes that Madame Bovary and other Flaubert characters "are marked by 'an essential lack of a fixed character and originality of their own . . . so that being *nothing* by themselves, they become *something*, one thing or another, through the suggestion which they obey.' These characters 'cannot equal the model they have chosen. Yet their vanity prevents them from admitting their failure'" (63). Like Madame Bovary, Emma turns briefly to religion in her youth in search of spiritual enlightenment, and, perhaps, in search of becoming Gaultier's "something." But, unlike Flaubert's character, she gives up the meaning-inscribed cultural models in favor of an emotional and libidinal excess that, while it ultimately will destroy Madame Bovary, allows Emma to create new and fluid identities that do not come pre-inscribed with acceptable cultural meanings. It is sadomasochistic play that creates, in Emma, the blank slate needed for the transcendence of these cultural models.

Emma and Claire, however, are not the only ones of Martin's characters to suffer from a need to find such transcendence. In her short story "The Woman Who Was Never Satisfied," Martin creates a woman, Eva, who literally needs to be *emptied* in order to feel fulfilled. Eva finds that the only time in her life she is peaceful is after having blood withdrawn from her via a syringe. She pays men with sex to have them draw blood from her and only then reaches a kind of calm that more closely resembles numbness than it does peace. Eva, however, believes it to be peace and is willing to pay "any price" for the feel of it (51). When she meets Lawrence, he takes away her need to feel that emptiness. He is an animal doctor who has dozens of animals in his home at all times. Through the caretaking of animals and by helping her new husband with all of the chores that must be done, she loses time too quickly to think about feeling irritated or unsatisfied, but after Lawrence dies, the lack of satisfaction comes back and she begins hunting down men to fulfill her blood-letting need. Finally, after having her blood drawn one night, she wanders through the neighborhood in a kind of numb trance only to find herself drawn into church by the music coming from inside. After going into the church, she has what amounts to a spiritual vision of herself holding a dead bird and enters into a moment of religious ecstasy, falling on the ground in the aisle while everyone watches her.

Eva believes herself to be in need of literal purification. The blood inside her needs to be removed. This seems an obvious physical analog to the emotional and/or mental pain that she is suffering. Something inside of her needs to come out, and she interprets this as a need to literally remove parts of herself. There is, in her obsessive need, a kind of reminiscence of the mystical saint. While emptiness can certainly imply a kind of numbness or loneliness, it can also imply the potential, or the readiness to be filled. In the case of the mystics, that fulfillment comes from union with Christ or some other form of divine consciousness. Eva seems, at least in one regard, similar to those mystics, particularly the Christian ones. Lawrence was the protector of animal-kind. His good works were the works of protecting a small, virtual world of creations. A Jesus figure, he offers salvation to Eva (the similarity to the biblical Eve is most likely intentional, as Martin tends to use her names to full advantage) by allowing her to partake of his works. Like Emma, working for the poor and sick within the quarantine zone, Eva goes sleepless for the sake of nursing a "sick Diana monkey" or feeding an ill bluejay bits of "boiled egg yolk" during the night (53). She is the Mary Magdalene to Lawrence's Christ, saved from prostitution (or, in this case, from obsession) by his presence. It is unsurprising, then, that her vision in the church is a vision of one of the animals who, through her own fault and negligence, she had let die. She remembers sitting, holding the dead bird in her hands, and having been "struck by the conviction that the force that had animated this cold body must still be somewhere about, still in the room" (56).

In this moment, thinking about this bird, Eva realizes that the spirit, or the animating force, is separate from the body, and this marks the turning point in her obsession with purifying her body in order to feel better about her spirit. She falls into a religious fever and drops to her knees, "her thoughts transported, her heart uplifted, oblivious of the cold and curious eyes that fled every corner of the room to settle on her kneeling, now her prostrate form" (57). The music, the same music that drove Murmur Lee into epileptic fits, Katie Cocker into feelings of love and safety, Bone into the pit of desire, and Claire into transcendent visions, allows Eva to finally understand, though the reader perhaps may not see it immediately, that her emptiness can have fulfillment. This is not to say that such fulfillment is not at least partially troubling. In the last moment before she falls into her religious trance, she sees the face of her husband and hears his voice in "the rising flood of music," intimating that the intensity of the music, the power of the service, fills her with the same fulfillment that her husband had. However, just below the surface of her "fulfillment" with her husband had been the realization that perhaps there was more to life than just doing his work, taking care of his animals, and helping his life. After all, it is right before he dies in a car crash that she can't help herself from momentarily wishing that "Lawrence and all his animals were dead" (54). John Irwin Fischer argues that in Martin's books and stories "masochism is a defence of the ego, not a willing surrender of it" (447), and in the cases where masochism and mysticism do the same work of creating identity, it seems he is right, but in Eva we see, much like in Claire, a character who has not quite made that leap yet. She instead seems only on the verge of understanding. Emptiness can lead to fulfillment, but not every fulfillment is productive.

Another character who seems on the verge of understanding the ways in which masochism can help create identity rather than efface it is Ellen, the protagonist of Martin's story "Surface Calm." Ellen, the wife of a successful businessman, begins to hurt herself with needles, razors, and garden shears after her husband leaves on a business trip. The amount of pain she inflicts upon herself grows daily as her husband is gone, and she finds herself both terrified and relieved by the bloodletting that occurs as a result. This story, one of many in a collection called simply *Love,* provides a fascinating look at a woman who suddenly finds, in self-masochism, an answer to the loneliness that lays just below the surface of her life. Ellen has lived an entirely protected and cloistered life, and she goes straight from her mother's house to her husband's house, where her daily routine is mapped out in terms of gardening, homemaking, and running errands. It is a life that seems to leave her fulfilled, but her reactions to her husband's business trip bring into question just how fulfilled she is. John Irwin Fischer explains that, while clinical definitions of masochism may help to explain some of the actions that Ellen takes, they do not explain all of them, including why Ellen feels better "'as soon as she was in the car and made the stops and turns that led to the grocery store as if she were a horse whose life was one routine'" or why society "regards her vacant life as normal" or finally "why, though her husband is horrified by her self-flagellation, 'though he was convinced that she was mad,' he still wished to make love to her, and does so" (447).

While there are undoubtedly multiple explanations, it seems that Ellen, like Emma, suffers not for complete self-annihilation but in order to feel alive—to give herself the intensity that reminds her she is *not* dead. Unlike Claire, who believes she has accepted death as a viable course in order to achieve sainthood, Ellen does not want death. Her life as she lives it, however, is a passive one. It is her husband who gives her life meaning, and she lives, like many a historically "good" southern woman, for his happiness, sacrificing any personal identity and desire for his own. The business of life, however, keeps her too preoccupied to notice that underneath the surface is a repressed loneliness. Once her husband is gone, it takes very little time for her to begin cutting herself.

If Ellen, like Eva, is currently "empty," then it is pain that she uses to fill herself. Emma calls sex "the great leveler," but in her works, more often than not, Martin uses pain as the great leveler. It can reduce, but it can also exalt—much like sex and/or religion. As we see in both Emma and Bone and, to a lesser extent, Claire, pain can be a way of claiming the body and taking it outside itself. If the pain is self-inflicted, then that pain, as Morris says, is a way of overcoming the body *through* the body. For Ellen, self-mutilation, whether it is poking herself with sewing needles or slicing her fingers with gardening shears, seems to hold the potential not only for bodily reclamation, but also for spiritual reclamation. Unfortunately, the story ends with the potential unrealized. When her husband comes home, she begins to take joy in cooking him meals, in submitting to his sexual desires (even when those desires are, troublingly, for her mutilated body), and in arranging her day around his in order to be with him. The daily life of a housewife seems to give her renewed strength and energy, but as soon as he leaves, she begins to hurt herself again. It is also significant that the tools she uses to hurt herself tend to be the same tools that she uses for the purpose of homemaking. Her gardening shears, her sewing needles, and a broken chain from an old lamp are the instruments of her livelihood and her self-inflicted pain. Although she certainly does not seem aware of it, Ellen seems to be telling herself that the same things that seem to make her happy are the very ones that are, under the surface, destroying her. If she understood this, the potential of the self-masochism could be fully realized. Instead, she knows only that, when she hurt herself, "she found herself laughing and crying in alternate bursts of fear and pleasure, anger and relief" (22). If Fischer is right and Martin does indeed understand that "masochism is a defence of the ego" (447), it is not something that Ellen understands, although her laughter, her pleasure, and her relief hint that she, too, is on the verge of that understanding.

In Sheri Reynolds's *The Rapture of Canaan* is a character who seems to both fully and consciously realize, in ways that the characters in this study generally do not (with the exception of Dorothy Allison), that masochism and self-inflicted pain can become a productive part of positive self-creation and identification. Although by the end of the novel Ninah Huff has given up hurting herself and has devoted herself to the raising of her son Canaan, she has not dismissed pain as an important site of growth. Pain is, however, not the *final* site of growth for Ninah; it is one step along the path towards spiritual and physical enlightenment, particularly in regards to the community around her. Before Ninah reaches this point of understanding, however, she too goes through a long process of trying to identify herself from the inside out. She, like Eva, seems to realize that there is something inside of her that is keeping her from happiness, and, like Eva, she would like to get rid of it if she could. Unlike Rosemary Daniell, who felt a secret "power" in the blood of her first menstrual cycle, Ninah is both saddened and ashamed by the blood that accompanies puberty. Oprah Winfrey, in a reading guide designed for the novel, calls Ninah's first menstrual cycle the "inciting moment" of this text, and there is a kind of truth to the claim.

Ninah herself claims, "It started with the bleeding," and it was "a change for the worse" (35). For Daniell, the power of womanhood is the very limited power of control over men through sex appeal and sex acts. If she can bleed, then she is a woman, and womanhood entails the ability to say yes or no to sex, thus controlling her partners' access to her body. As she gets older, Daniell will use this power over and over both to make herself feel stronger and to exert power over the men (and later women) that she chooses to be with, but this is a tricky power because it is the power of the object and not the power of the subject. As pointed out by Jessica Benjamin in her critical work *The Bonds of Love,* such "power" derives completely from the ability to be seen and desired as object by the viewer. A "sexy woman," Benjamin writes, "expresses not so much *her* desire as her pleasure in being desired; what she enjoys is her capacity to evoke desire in the other, to attract," and this power cannot "be described as the power of a sexual subject" (89). Ninah, as if sensing this very point, finds no power in the coming of her womanhood. In fact, as she looks around her at the girls and women in her community, she realizes that even this limited power may not exist for her for multiple reasons. The first of these reasons is that, through a series of strict regulations and commandments, the community has all but denied women the ability to control access to their own bodies. If a man has sex with a woman to whom he is not married, he will suffer punishments ranging from paying fees to the husbands/fathers of the women to suffering "dunking," or being buried overnight in a grave. Such punishments, medieval in flavor and structure, serve to curtail extramarital sex, and place sexual decisions into the hands of the men of the community. Further, women, once married, belong bodily to their husbands.

It isn't just the sexual limitations put on members of the congregation, however, that keep Ninah from even the power of the "sexy woman," it is also that everyone looks the same—there is nothing to distinguish her physically from the other girls in the compound: "We may as well have been skeletons, unidentifiable. . . . I used to pray that God would stunt my growth and keep me little—so at least my frame wouldn't be confused with anyone else's" (37–38). Womanhood thus appears to involve not just objectification, but a categorization of all girls into a similar role. Like other girls in the community, she will grow up to become a caretaker, a cook, a mother, and a sexual object without the power even to control access to her own body. This fact certainly seems partially responsible for the fascination that Ninah finds in the sexual exploits of girls who live outside of her community. It isn't just the sex acts themselves that interest her, but the attempts to become sexually alluring—buying makeup and perfume, wearing different clothing, and talking with "attitude" all draw her consideration. Like those girls by whom she is intrigued, Ninah wants to have some control over how she is seen and who sees her. She wants to force people to see her as an individual object and not one of many, not part of a string of "paper dolls" (37). This understanding is Ninah's first step towards subjecthood and feminine power, but ultimately Ninah's real power will not come through embracing objectification, as Benjamin's "sexy woman" does. Instead, it will come through rebellion against the authoritarian, patriarchal religious system set up by her grandfather; it will come through the creation of art that incorporates all aspects of her life, and it will come through the use of pain as a method of both relating to religion and finding a new connection to spirituality.

In his study *Sacred Pain: Hurting the Body for the Sake of the Soul*, Ariel Glucklich examines the ways in which pain can be transformed into "meaningful religious experience" (78) and some of the reasons why and methods by which people have historically used self-inflicted or voluntary pain to achieve a desired state of mind. Generally speaking, these "states of mind" are negative ones. As discussed by Glucklich, Morris, and others, physical torment has traditionally been used religiously to empty the mind of temptation, sinful thoughts, or even thoughts of the self. As self-negation is important in the quest for transcendent or mystical states, self-inflicted pain, starvation, or even (in the case of some of the Christian mystics) purposeful exposure to disease has been used to achieve that state. Loss of the self, through pain or other forms of punishment or self-denial, prepared an individual to be filled with the divine instead.

Of course, the complication, as Underhill has pointed out, is that, because attention is drawn to the physical body in order to forget the physical body altogether, such manipulations as self-flagellation or self-exposure to pain and disease may in fact be a sublimated response to a desire that comes from the "lower centres" of the body rather than from spiritual enlightenment. Describing mystical ascetic practices in this ego-annihilating way definitely seems to align them with sadomasochistic practices, as commonly defined by psychoanalysis, with its desire for obliteration of the self. The difference between the two seems to reside in what comes next—for the mystic, self-negation is a step towards fulfillment from the divine whereas for the masochist, the self-negation seems, if we believe Freud, to be the very point. Of course, both of these claims simplify the matter since there is a point beyond the divine and beyond the self-negation, and that point is the pleasure derived from the acts of either divine fulfillment or masochism—that is, reaching a place of peace, or finding ecstasy.

For Ninah, a movement towards ecstasy involves attempts at both pain and religious self-negation. Glucklich argues that pain "is neither a simple biological event—say, tissue damage—nor an idea. It occupies a space 'in between,' a middle-of-the-road phenomenal position between the material organism and the mind" (9).[5] Ninah certainly provides an example of this interstitial pain that connects the mind to the material. When she realizes that she is feeling "flutters" for James, and her father tells her "physical discomfort is one of the best ways to keep your mind on Heaven" (61), she takes his advice to heart and begins a regimen of self-inflicted pain in an attempt to forget about her feelings: "I decided to concentrate on Jesus' pain as hard as I could. I put sandspurs in my own bed and pecan shells in my shoes to remind me with every step of how Jesus had suffered. I cut out a picture of Jesus on the cross and taped it to the inside of my underwear for protection—because if I was saving myself for Jesus, I knew I'd better get him there fast" (74).

Although Grandpa Herman and her father have both recommended such self-inflicted pain to the congregation, the suffering that Ninah does seems to call Ninah's attention less to the suffering of Jesus than to the physicality of such suffering. That she wears a picture of Jesus in her underwear and a clothespin on each nipple only brings focus to the erotic nature of her self-punishments. She is attempting to silence those areas of her physical body that she sees as causing her the most trouble—attempting to negate these areas by drawing physical attention to them, but by irritating these areas, she only draws her own attention to those same areas.

Rather than seeing this as a negative thing, however, Reynolds seems to be showing readers that pain provides Ninah with one of the first bridges between her spirituality and sexuality by allowing her to apply one to the other. Further evidence of this is apparent when Ninah later exchanges her physical torments for sexual activities that she declares to be holy in nature. If we view her early experiments with pain as masochistic in nature, an attempt to negate areas of her body through pain inflicted upon them, then her later experiments with sex seem to move more toward mysticism. In a description of sex between James and Ninah, Ninah explores the idea of a mystical fulfillment that she believes occurs: "Jesus just whirlwinded around inside of me until he got so big that he started slipping out, and I think it happened the same with James. Jesus just filled us up, so full we had to share it. It wasn't fornication. Not there, with the tobacco leaves lisping in the warm wind, not with the moon overhead like a spotlight so that God could see from way up there" (140).

Her description of Jesus as filling her completely definitely reso- nates with stories and descriptions of mysticism, especially those of the mystics such as Catherine of Siena and Teresa of Avila, whose mystical unions with Christ would first fill them up and then rush out of them, leaving them exhausted and spent. But these moments of mystical union lose their transcendence once she realizes that James doesn't really be- lieve that Jesus is a part of their lovemaking, and once more she turns to the self-infliction of pain, wearing hair shirts, walking with pecan shells in her shoes, and wrapping barbed wire around her stomach. In addition, she begins having dreams about "being whipped in front of the alter" by James, who was "whipping me, then rolling over and being Jesus for me, except he wasn't Jesus. He was Satan. Either Satan or Grandpa Herman" (149). This dream reflects her guilt at having had sex not with Jesus, but with James. When it was Jesus, it was a holy act, but now that she knows the truth, she believes that the act was a sinful one, and that it was Satan driving her and her grandfather judging her (although the combination of Satan with her grandfather shows that, even in the midst of her guilt, she knows that her ideas of sin are constructed through the rules and regulations of her grandfather, rather than through any organic or super- natural knowledge of sin).

The dreams that she is having and the pain that she is inflicting, how- ever, do more than reflect her guilt—they continue to provide a bridge between her sexuality, her spirituality, and her community. Morris points out that "the religious and prophetic uses of pain . . . stand in conflict with almost all ordinary ways of seeing" and "demand a full-scale reinterpretation of the everyday world" and that "pain has long served as a bridge . . . between entirely different realms of value" (125). Ninah is eager for such a reinterpretation of her life and her surroundings, and pain provides her the catalyst for change in thought. It *is* the bridge between these different aspects of her world, and that pain is most graphically represented by the art she creates. (One is reminded of Gearheart's statement that "art, like sado-masochism, may involve the transformation of pain into pleasure.") The dream that it is her grandfather having sex with her and whipping her points to the fear of his authoritarian regime, but also to the fear of that regime's control over her sexuality. He, as representative of religion, has always had control over her sexuality, either through his prohibitions or through the culturally imposed guilt that both James and Ninah feel. The dream is thus her only outlet for fear and guilt until she begins creating her rugs.

It is only after beginning her artwork, and after she realizes that she is pregnant, that the dreams begin to change to reflect her new understanding of the relationship between sex and spirituality. In her postpregnancy dreams, she still imagines Jesus as a partner, but now it is a Jesus who, while on the cross, holds out azaleas to court her. Azaleas were the flowers with which her grandfather had courted her grandmother, and so in her dream image, Ninah reconfigures her connection to the different realms of her everyday existence. In the first dream, she is being whipped in front of an altar, suffering punishment for some religious offense (most likely her sexual guilt, as reflected by James's presence in the dream), whereas in the second dream, it is Jesus who suffers, as evinced by his position on the cross. Jesus, however, is glad to be suffering—this is the traditional image of Jesus as the sacrificial figure, yet he is still courting her with the same azaleas her grandfather once used during his youth, when his religious rigidity was perhaps a little looser. Instead of making a correlation between her grandfather and Satan, she now makes that same connection between her grandfather and Jesus. She is seeing, perhaps for the first time, the ways in which her grandfather, far from being simply a monstrous figure of authority, is also human. Although this dream, unlike the alienating first dream, provides for her a bridge to the community, to her sexuality, and to her spirituality, she does still associate her grandfather with one of the ultimate patriarchal religious figures, it's just that she is beginning to understand that Jesus (like her grandfather) is perhaps a little more yielding than she might have once thought. She is also beginning to connect to religion through a positive spirituality that provides her pleasure and beauty (as represented by the azaleas *and* the courting gesture). Her self-inflicted pain, her creation of art, and now her visionary dreams have all given her the capabilities of understanding, if not yet seeing, that there is something beyond what she knows. Like Bone, Ninah is becoming aware of the mystical nature of her own sexuality.

The understanding that there is something spiritual about her sexuality and about the physical world around her is shown in Ninah's reevaluation of her community after she gets pregnant. Even though Herman attempts to exert control over Ninah's very flesh by keeping her cloistered away from the community, Ninah bucks this control and leaves the house despite being warned against it. As she wanders past the houses, she starts to feel as if she is waking up from something, and as she continues through the "coldness, the winter smell of firewood smoldering out chimneys and the sound of pine needles half frozen and tinkling in the wind" (215), she realizes that for the first time she feels good about her community and that there are positive aspects to a communal way of life. Her memories during this walk are happy ones, as opposed to the repressive ones of her early walk through the community wherein all she could see were the ways in which everyone was alike—all paper dolls cut from the same mold. This interaction or communion with the world around her that includes not only her family and neighbors but also the natural world of the winter and the trees and the "coldness" is her way of waking up to the mystical nature of the world. Often in mystical testimonies, a feeling of coldness, or a cold wind is described as being one of the signs of the oncoming of a spiritual moment, particularly a moment of ecstasy or understanding, and for Ninah, this is no exception, but her moment of understanding is delayed until after the birth of her son.

When Canaan is born, his hands fused together in a pose resembling prayer, the community is convinced that Ninah was not lying—that the baby is in fact the child of Christ and thus holy. For a while, even Ninah is re-convinced, believing that perhaps she really "was knowing Jesus and not James" (241). Still, she knows better and, furthermore, no longer needs this lie to escape the guilt, and so she ultimately gives up the belief that Jesus had been a part of her and James's lovemaking. This does not, however, mean that she gave up the idea that her lovemaking had been holy. In fact, the sanctity of sex and the body is something that Ninah has slowly learned to accept, and when she becomes the new "Virgin Mary" to the community, she takes advantage of it to attempt to make changes regarding the physical body. She begins to cut the women's hair and to encourage others to wear pants or other clothes that make them comfortable, and she objects to them leaving Canaan's hands fused together. She is disheartened by Canaan's hands because she understands that they give Herman's teachings credence and that, as long as his hands are fused, Canaan will be relegated to the prescribed role of holy child, inundated with expectations, and treated as a physical manifestation of only the spiritual, to the exclusion of the physical. His body, she knows, will become no more than a symbol—the same way women's bodies have been seen all along. Ninah's new understanding of the spiritual in her life incorporates the body in all of its beauty and ugliness, as evinced by the rugs that she creates, and she is eventually pushed to cut Canaan's hands apart because she does not want her child forced to fill the role of a Messiah who will only keep her community in the same place it has always been, trapped by superstition and strict rules that regulate the very bodies of its members.

CHAPTER 5

Contemporary Repercussions

> Ladies, get ACTIVE in church. Attend church as often as those doors open.
> Get busy. You will hopefully be noticed and approached by a Godly man
> who admires your walk and obvious love of God.
> —www.christianwomen.net/marriage.html

> If you didn't have the vision before you married to look for a man of God,
> you can still pray that God will transform the man you married.
> —DEE BRESTIN, *Falling in Love with Jesus*

Feminists have long argued about the place of religion in women's lives
and, since the 1960s, have been arguing in particular about the place of
theology in feminism. In fact, the term "feminist theology" is standard
enough now that Cambridge University Press released, in 2002, *The
Cambridge Companion to Feminist Theology*, an anthology dealing with
its history and its place in the broader contexts of both feminism and
theology. In it, some of the most influential scholars of feminist theology summarized, criticized, and discussed the ways in which theology
has traditionally (and non-traditionally) been viewed through the lens of
feminism. In particular, the essays included are concerned with the very
issues that plague the texts in this study—concepts of love and desire,
the roles of faith and submission (especially female submission), and the
gendering of religious expression and symbols.

   In the opening essay, "The Emergence of Christian Feminist Theology," Rosemary Ruether, perhaps the best-known voice in feminist theology, delineates the most common reactions of feminists to Christian

theology and to Christianity in general. These reactions, she argues, can be summed up generally into three categories—those of feminists such as Carol Christ who "concluded that patriarchy is too deeply entrenched in this tradition to be capable of feminist transformation" (11) and have turned away from any traditional forms of Christianity; those of theorists and theologians such as Susan Ross who are interested in the ways that women work within traditional forms of Christianity while "reshaping" traditional Christian symbols and teachings to include and value women and women's experiences; and those of "separatists" who argue for a separate women's church that takes, as its basis for religion, women's experiences outside and/or above the experiences of men. Ruether argues, however, that despite these differences and despite the (at times) seeming lack of cohesion amongst Christian women theologians, all "are concerned with common themes of critique of sexist symbols in Christianity and the reconstruction of the symbolism for God, Christ, humanity and nature, sin, and salvation, to affirm women's full and equivalent humanity" (18). The *Cambridge Companion* takes this as its starting point for discussion of how women seek to interpret the divine and their own roles in the naming, worshipping and understanding of it/him/her.

Although the understandings and discussions of feminist theology that exist, especially as represented in the anthology, do not always speak to the situations and problems presented by the authors in this study, all of our characters and authors find and articulate various methods for understanding and coping with the Christian divine, including all three of the above strategies, and combinations thereof. In the work of Daniell, for example, there is a decided antagonism towards the place of organized Christian religion in the South, particularly where women's roles are concerned. At the same time, however, Daniell has a great deal of respect for and fascination with the symbols of Christianity, particularly Catholicism. Mary stands as the most obvious example, because she appears time and again in the author's works as a mother, a lover, and even as the "sucker" who was used to propagate a patriarchal religion that would attempt to control her very own body. In this way, Daniell's treatment of religion is similar to that of Lee Smith, who finds in Christian faith, traditions, and sacraments, symbols that can provide meaning and/or inspiration for women, even if not in the ideologically prescribed ways.

When Grace takes up hot coals, as her mother did, there is a very real sense that, while she is performing the same ritual as countless others before her, she is reinventing this act as sacramental in a new way—in a way that may celebrate not only the feminine spirit, but the female body itself. She is not immune to the heat of the coals because God has protected her, but because she has been led to these coals by the spirit of her mother, who becomes a divine figure for Grace. This episode calls to mind the moment in Jacob and Wilhelm Grimm's "Cinderella" wherein Cinderella's real mother sends her dresses and shoes from beyond the grave in order to help her achieve her place in life. That this scene draws upon both religious imagery and fairy tales speaks volumes about the influences most likely to impact girls' understandings about what it means to be female, particularly in the South. In fact, references to fairy-tale "princesses" and other fairy-tale elements resonate throughout the body of Smith's works, offering a site of gender/identity creation. In *Saving Grace,* however, while these moments seem to challenge the notion of a dominant patriarchal ideology, they also and predominantly underscore the traditional gender roles associated with fairy tales.

In her essay from the *Cambridge Companion,* however, Susan A. Ross offers the idea that "women's preaching has the power to break open the word of God, *naming grace* in ways that have until now gone unspoken" (232). Such a claim offers an interesting interpretation of Grace's journey through that novel. As Rebecca Smith points out, one of the predominant themes throughout *Saving Grace* is the power of naming—Grace even begins the narrative by telling readers, "My name is Florida Grace Shepherd, Florida for the state I was born in, Grace for the Grace of God" (3). Through the telling of her story, which is also her testimonial, she has become a preacher, and she is both literally and figuratively "naming grace" in a way that has not been done before, at least not in the examples of preaching and testimony found in this book and others of Smith's. Grace tells readers, "I am a believer in the Word, and I am not going to flinch from telling it, not even the terrible things. . . . I have entered these dark woods yet again, for I've got to find out who I am and what has happened to me, so that I can understand what is happening to me now, and what is going to happen to me next" (4). Unlike the other, patriarchal testimonies of the text, hers is one that is not done, but is still *in the process* of being undergone, even as she tells it.

Unlike Smith and Daniell, who are able to find within Christianity a reinvention of traditional symbols, Connie May Fowler's Bird is ultimately dismissive of religion, understanding that there is nothing in Jesus that can save her from very real, material conditions of abuse and poverty and that, in God's relationship with humanity, there is only a mimetic version of the parent-child relationship, which she finds frightening and demoralizing. While Grace also associates Jesus with a parent figure, Grace learns to reassign Jesus from parent to child, relating to him first as a daughter, then as a spouse, and finally as a mother. It is through motherhood that Grace finds something worthwhile in believing in Jesus. Bird, however, never reaches that point. She knows, instead, that Jesus cannot help her because his own father is no better to him than her mother is to her. Of course, Bone from *Bastard Out of Carolina* would have to agree with Bird that Jesus seems unable to help in any real sense, but Bone is also, without knowing the language for it, looking for and even believing in the kind of transcendence that Bird has dismissed as impossible. It is not in Jesus that Bone places her faith, but in the power of the mind and, like Grace, the power of testimony. As long as Bone can tell her stories, even the ones she tells to herself in private, she has the power to temporarily escape, at least mentally, her abuse, and to permanently, over time, escape victimhood as a state of being. What religion offers Bone is a way of normalizing yearning that is safer than romantic or sexual yearning. Religion allows for a yearning *toward* faith; it creates a threshold at the moment of being saved and a liminal place where nothing is concrete, where God and the Devil are struggling for the soul. This is a place where the act of *becoming* is vital, and as long as a decision is in the *process* of being made, hope still exists. It is this hope, this belief in the ability to transcend the current state, that makes Bone the young would-be mystic.

Martin's characters are would-be mystics as well, but they are grounded mystics for whom transcendence represents an ultimately unattainable goal, one that is nonetheless worthy of trying to attain. The act of sex, much like the act of prayer, is a way to that transcendence, and the act itself, the "falling," as Martin calls it, is worth the attempt because of the doors that it opens from the soul into the world. While Claire is unable to connect to humanity, Emma finds the power to do so only because she is able to transcend the trivialities of her own life and egoistic urges. Martin's theological views seem to follow closely those of Carol

Christ, who argues that the work of all feminist theologians is to replace "dualistic thinking . . . with more holistic models" (86), and also those of some of the early liberation theologists who believed in looking at the Catholic liturgy through the lens of the disenfranchised, particularly in third-world countries. Though New Orleans is not a third-world country, as it is depicted by Martin in *A Recent Martyr* (the streets are plague ridden, and the people hope for miracles), it certainly shares similarities. It is ultimately through working with the poor that Emma realizes her own connection to humanity, understanding that Pascal's hands-off approach to other human beings leaves him jaded and pessimistic, and it is this pessimism that leads to despair—the one thing that will forever bar her from transcending her own ego to merge with the divine, humanity, or even a mortal partner. The "holistic model" proposed by Martin in this and other works is a model that involves intimacy, eroticism, and sensual experience, allowing for the merging of the sexual and the sacred rather than its compartmentalization.

The theology of Sheri Reynolds's *Rapture of Canaan* reflects the work of those theorists who find in Christianity a philosophy worthy of following, but only after a radical rethinking of the forces that inspire and create faith itself. Ninah's beliefs in the sacred eroticism that she shares with James seem to be exactly what theologian Nicola Slee is talking about when she writes that "there is a strong emphasis on *desire, eros,* and *passion* in much contemporary feminist spirituality which may be seen as a reconceptualisation of the Spirit's work of inspiring, energizing and enlivening faith in ways which take seriously the human body, emotions, and drives" (179). Ninah, however, is not alone in her creation of a new feminist spirituality through which to view the world around her.

Ultimately, all of these women, authors as well as characters, work towards an understanding of faith that incorporates the body and its pleasures and pains. Ninah, like Grace, learns to re-relate to religion through motherhood and finds peace only after becoming the new "Mary" for the community in which she lives. In that way, she also shares with Daniell a fascination with the symbolic nature of Mary as a religious figure who is mother, daughter, and lover to the divine. Ninah also resembles, through her focus on bodily sensations, the characters in Dorothy Allison and Valerie Martin's novels who find in self-inflicted pain avenues towards understanding, reconciliation with themselves, and transcendence both of bodily abuse and victimhood. Finally, in Lee Smith's Katie Cocker, we see another analog to Ninah in a woman whose creation of art as a means of encapsulating both the sacred and the sexual leads to a renewed understanding of both. For Katie, that art is music while for Ninah it is rug weaving, but in both instances, real and imagined heterotopic spaces provide physical and emotional fulfillment.

All of the above have spent time in the liminal space between the sexual and the sacred. For some, it is a space of growth, and they are able to create a place that can contain all of those opposite meanings at once without seeming contradiction. This study has focused primarily on literary and historical theory as an underpinning for the creation of these literary spaces, but I want now to turn to some of the more contemporary and practical results of the kinds of theological practices in which our subjects are engaged. It is, of course, easy to speak of the southern woman as if she were an artifact of the past, a historical construction, or a theoretical simulacrum. Although it seems common to discuss "The South" and its various inhabitants in terms of imagined communities and shared identifications (and I have certainly done so), there are also very real, material moments occurring in the South that speak to the theoretical and critical materials.

In its influence on women and their relation to sex and Christianity in the South, the creation of the mega-church and all of its attendant communities is almost without rival. Although mega-churches are not unique to the South, the South certainly has an abundance of them. Of the 1,366 mega-churches listed in the Hartford Institute for Religious Study's database of mega-churches in North America, 418 (30 percent) are located in the thirteen southern states of Alabama, Arkansas, Florida, Georgia, Kentucky, Louisiana, Mississippi, North Carolina, South Carolina, Tennessee, and Virginia. Factoring in another 207 located in the border states of Maryland, Texas, and West Virginia, the total number in and around the South is 625, or 45 percent of all mega-churches in North America. The mega-church's influence is most widely felt in southern evangelical religions, including the Methodist and Southern Baptist faiths. The mega-church has literally and figuratively changed the landscape of southern religion, offering up charismatic leaders whose churches contain everything from gymnasiums to beauty parlors to grocery stores.

By making the church into a material as well as a spiritual community, church leaders and administrators have helped religion to reclaim a place of vital importance not only in the lives of the individual parishioners, but also in the community. Because each mega-church generally has over 3,000 members, these churches are literal forces for political, social, and cultural movement. Their extensive influence and large communities normalize the practices of its members so that what might seem questionable in a group of 20 to 200 suddenly seems to be quite rational simply by virtue of numbers. As well, peer-driven groups within the various churches help focus the religious direction of the community while, at the same time, they help solidify the overarching ideology of the churches in question. Among these peer groups are women who often hold weekly scheduled events and/or meetings for singles, teenage girls, mothers, brides-to-be, and even married women whose marriages are suffering. These various groups often do the job of confirming the place of religion in the lives of women while at the same time confirming Christianity's patriarchal structure.

Sociologist Michelle Wolkomir, in studying one such peer group, was able to support just such an understanding. Exodus International, a Christian ministry that specializes in helping to reform and/or help homosexual Christians, has relationships with many of the Protestant mega-churches in the South, where it offers training and help for a variety of support groups such as the one Wolkomir studied, which provided help for women of (primarily) ex-gay husbands. The women who attended these support groups were, understandably, concerned about issues relating not just to their husbands' sexuality, but to their own as well. The groups, according to Wolkomir, "did help the women develop successful coping strategies that at times included acts of resistance," but ultimately, these strategies, she argues, "were constructed to fit within ideological parameters established by the support groups and to reaffirm these boundaries." Among these were gender boundaries that stressed "men's leadership" and "protected existing gender ideologies and configurations of practice" (753). The primary strategy that served both the needs of the women and the needs of the dominant patriarchal ideology presented by the church was a strategy of total submission to God. Wolkomir points out that, because submission to their husbands was problematic, the wives were taught that they "should circumvent their 'sick' husbands and submit wholly to God, the preeminent masculine authority" (747). Submission allowed the women to "regain control of their lives only by giving up control and relying on a masculine God to give them directions" (748).

It's not hard to see the similarities between this strategy of surrender to a male God and the actions of many of the characters throughout this study. For these women, "submitting to God was also a transformative act, enabling [them] to redefine their identities and reconstruct once shameful marriages into sites for sacred work" (749), and for characters such as Bone, Emma, and Claire, complete submission, whether to a divine presence, a mortal man, or just to a fantasy of fire, is also transformative, allowing them to redefine themselves as non-victim, part of humanity, or as mystical saint. As well, these wives, by "circumventing" their husbands to seek out more definite relationships with the divine, are engaging in just the same sort of relationship strategies as Daniell, Ninah, and Bird, creating in God and/or Jesus an alternative partner in whose strength they place not only their faith, but also their desire. Even in a group aimed at helping women with "sick" husbands whose authority is questioned, the dominant Christian lessons of sacrifice and religious support are upheld. Southern Baptist women were taught through lectures, sermons, classes, and informal groups that "the issue of wifely obedience" is still important and that women should "make their husbands (better) Christians by manifesting a quiet, gentle spirit" (Pevey, Williams, and Ellison 142). This is exactly the lesson being taught to the women in Wolkomir's study who are instructed to give up authority, to be obedient to a male authority figure, and to help their husbands through their own sacrifices and "quiet, gentle" spirits.

Although such lessons are not limited strictly to mega-churches, in the last decade there has also been a resurgence in such cultural artifacts as chastity promises, purity balls, and abstinence groups. Aimed primarily at teenage girls, purity balls have become big business for big churches. In general, at these dances, fathers escort their daughters and, at chosen times, present their daughters with "promise rings" that indicate the daughters will be "faithful" to the promise of chastity—a promise made to their literal fathers and to the divine father as well. Despite the eerily incestuous undertones to these balls, they are not far removed from traditional weddings wherein fathers give their daughters away. Underlying both traditions is the idea that a daughter belongs first to her father and then, eventually, to her husband. The women in Wolkomir's group, then, can be seen in some ways as returning to their fathers' houses by removing their obedience from their husbands and returning them to the divine father. Above all, these purity balls and chastity promises offer alternatives to similar secular entertainments. From Christian rock concerts to Christian teen groups, the activities of teen girls can be mimicked in the churches—especially the larger churches. Offering everything from gymnasiums to pool halls to beauty parlors, the modern large church can replicate in a religious environment what has traditionally been found only in the secular community, and the Christian values and ideologies become normalized through the power of peer support.

Another arena which has changed the shape of women's faith in the twenty-first century is the Internet. Of course the Internet has changed everything from the way we shop to how we meet new people, and the very idea of community has grown in a wireless world where "cyberborders" are pretty much nonexistent. One change that has taken place is that many ministries and churches have strictly or at least predominantly online congregations. Two such ministries worth note are the Fireproof Ministries, creators of XXXChurch.com and the "Jesus Loves Porn Stars" Bible, and the Christian Women for Jesus Ministries whose website offers advice for women, relevant scriptural lessons, and even online salvation through the repetition of a saving prayer and a quick email. The XXXChurch's mission (or X3 as they call themselves), according to the website, is "to make you think, react and to decide where you stand on the issues of porn." It is, they say, both "provocative" and "memorable," and it "combines the seedy and the sacred." The church publishes Bibles with bright pink and yellow covers that read "Jesus Loves Porn Stars," to give out at adult expositions and other sex-industry events.[1] While it is aimed primarily at those working in the sex industry, it has garnered quite a following through its internet presence, and the majority of its financing comes from online donations. According to one admirer of the church who posted in a review blog, the work that the church leaders are doing mimics the work of Jesus himself: "These are the kinds of people Jesus hung out with when He walked the earth. And that's what these guys are doing!" Through a focus on the biblical Jesus' life, on his compassion for prostitutes and other sinners, X3 has ostensibly used sex to "sell" Jesus. They even advertise themselves as the "#1 Christian Porn Site"—undoubtedly a strategy used to snag those seeking out porn sites with browsers or just to appeal to the prurient curiosity of those who see and/or hear about them. They are aware, as their site indicates, of the necessity of looking at bodily eroticism and religion together—to determine the necessary steps for defining each of them separately and combined. Whether X3 would agree with the authors this study examines is certainly questionable, but they definitely provide proof that such concerns exist even in the "real world" outside of literature.

Another ministry that exists primarily in the imagined space of the Internet is the Christian Women for Jesus ministries. This ministry's primary means of reaching its intended congregations is its website, at which women can find scriptural readings pertaining to the concerns of women in the twenty-first century and advice on how to live in a secular world while still following the proper (gendered) lifestyle as taught by the Bible. The mission of the Christian Women for Jesus ministries, according to their website, is "to edify, educate, and facilitate the growth and maturity of women from all walks of life, particularly women in transition from shelters, welfare, incarceration, halfway houses, poverty, and situations of abuse." Fittingly, this ministry strives to help those women who are *in transition,* without a definite space or place, just as the ministry itself is without a particular physical church. On the website, women are able to find advice in a range of areas that include the sexual and the religious. Among the pieces of advice offered to women who visit the site is that getting a man is easy—one only has to go to church. "Ladies," the site advises, "get ACTIVE in church. Attend church as often as those doors open." And in the next sentence, the motivation for getting ACTIVE becomes clear: "You will hopefully be noticed and approached by a Godly man who admires your walk *and* obvious love of God" (emphasis mine). This Godly man, obviously heterosexual (although the women of Wolkomin's group might disagree), will be sexually attracted to you *and* will notice your spiritual assets as well.

And, lest readers think this is the only example of using sexual and romantic desires to sell Jesus, all one needs to do is walk through a Christian bookstore or the Christian section of a major bookstore to see all of the books that attempt to appeal to women through their romantic and sexual desires. One book in particular is Dee Brestin and Kathy Troccoli's

Falling in Love With Jesus: Abandoning Yourself to the Greatest Romance of Your Life which makes explicit its agenda to show how loving Jesus is similar to and sometimes the same as loving a mortal man (only better!). By comparing the diary entries of a woman in love with the writing of a woman who has recently been saved, Brestin attempts to tell the story of "the Greatest Romance" possible for a woman. The subtitle, "Abandoning Yourself to the Greatest Romance of Your Life," brings to mind the cultural expectation that women will "abandon" themselves to love and to their lovers, submitting not just to their partners but to the overwhelming emotions that take them over. The reference to abandonment is significant because it evokes the kind of absolute submission that the women in Wolkomir's group were asked to offer to God, but also because of its romantic connotations. Simone de Beauvoir suggests that abandon can become "sacred ecstasy" because "[w]hen she *receives* her beloved, woman is dwelt in, visited, as was the Virgin by the Holy Ghost" and posits that "it is not that mystical love always has a sexual character, but that the sexuality of the woman in love is tinged with mysticism" (649). If secular women can abandon themselves to love, the argument seems to go, then holy women can achieve the same emotional intensity by simply abandoning themselves to love of the divine, and in this abandonment, there is always a touch of mysticism—of complete surrender.

If religion has often been seen in the South as the appropriate domain of women, then men have obviously, traditionally, been expectantly less involved in spiritual matters, and as a result, the very idea of religion and spirituality becomes associated with the feminine. One way that religion can and often is "masculinized," though, is through a focus on actual physical pain and punishment. Men are traditionally supposed to be able to handle more pain, more shock to the body. Like Christ, they will suffer through attacks on the body with relative silence. We especially see, in *Rapture of Canaan*, how the doling out of punishments and the defining of "Pain" become a male prerogative and how, when men are dealt punishment, they suffer it in silence. Ben Harback, for example, spends a night in an open grave as punishment for having extramarital sex but refuses to discuss or criticize the punishment.

The idea of a "masculinized" Christ has become increasingly popular over the years, particularly in the last years of the millennium when Christian men's groups proliferated, and the inclusion of gymnasiums or gym memberships as part of a church membership became fairly common in larger Protestant churches. Billboards such as the one that has a picture of Jesus in a thorny crown and reads "Meek. Mild. As If." were not uncommon to see in southern towns. Images of Jesus as a buff hero who could survive the physical torments of the world became a common advertising method for churches and ministries attempting to reach out to their male parishioners. Such tactics seems to posit an interesting counter to the idea that women are more able to relate to Jesus because of suffering, but upon closer inspection, the two ideas are not really at odds. For women, it is the act of suffering itself that draws them closer to Jesus—Jesus suffers constantly, as evinced by the images of him on the cross or carrying the cross or wearing a crown of thorns. As Jesus suffers, so too do women, but, for men, the suffering is something to be *overcome* or *endured*. What draws men to images of this masculine Jesus is that he is somehow strong enough to endure and fight the suffering, and the physical strength of Jesus is as important as the mental strength—this is perhaps why the logo of the Christian-owned Lord's Gym is a muscled Jesus bench-pressing the cross.

For women, on the other hand, it is the suffering itself that seems to draw them. Just as Bone was fascinated with the act of becoming something new, not the something new itself, women seem to relate to the constant act of suffering. This, of course, is a simplification and falls prey to arguments (rightfully so) that the idea is too essentializing, but it is a useful way to look at how these female characters view themselves in relation to Jesus, and the ways in which the various gendered ideals regarding Jesus break down along masculine/feminine lines in terms of strength versus passivity. Pain becomes a gendered object, one that is viewed differently when suffered by women or by men, and when caused by women or by men. While men may focus on the acts of punishment and ultimate redemption *through* pain, women seem to focus on the act of pain itself, on the redeeming qualities of suffering for the sake of suffering.

The eroticization of religion makes sense when identity construction is done against a backdrop of intense religious and sexual mores, rules, and laws. In a society where we are still prudishly adhering to laws laid down by the Puritans and Pilgrims three hundred years ago, it's not surprising that we sublimate our sexual yearnings into religious ones. It isn't much of a leap to see how religious yearnings can thus become sexual ones. This is especially prevalent in the South where, as Flannery O'Connor writes, the very landscape is "Christ Haunted" and where the most famous authors and artists are either overtly religious or dealing, in some way, with religion. In the work of the authors under discussion, we have seen how gender, sexuality, southernness, and, perhaps most importantly, desire have collided or colluded with faith and religion.

Just as authors and characters attempt to map out the spatial realms of their own desires, this text has mapped their mapping, looking at the effects of desire and what happens when desire is indulged and/or thwarted. Rosemary Daniell and Lee Smith trace the shape of controlled and frustrated desire not just in their own lives or the lives of their characters, but in the lives of southern women throughout time. Valerie Martin's work examines the space where desires become obsessions, and novels by Sheri Reynolds examine that same desire when the objects of desire turn out to be something other than originally thought and lead the desiring subject to new understandings of themselves. Finally, in works by Allison and Fowler, women are wrongly seen by themselves and often by others to be beyond all but the most domestic or basic forms of desire (desire for food, shelter, and so forth).

What all of these authors have in common, however, is that they employ and examine desire in ways that show it to be complicated and multifaceted. Desire is the guiding force of their lives and provides the motivations for actions that often seem, on the surface, bizarre or unusual, particularly when sexual desire is found in tandem with or competing against religious desire. These women have been able to carve out spaces for themselves that, while not denying anger, guilt, anxiety, depression, and/or inexplicable hungers and cravings, allow for the creation of meaning and identity. The question each of these authors and characters, or for that matter, any "southern" woman must ask herself becomes whether religion in the South can serve as a positive force in a woman's life, or exist along with a positive sexuality, and if it can, whether negative influences and effects can be overcome in order to make it so. It is important that, when these questions are asked, they be asked without limiting the power and potentiality of either religion or sexuality. What these authors seem to say is that, despite the teachings of southern patriarchy, and despite the formation of a hegemonic "southern woman" identity, real women in the South achieve psychic and psychological health only when eroticism and spirituality can be viewed both independently and in combination, and only when neither is relegated to an inferior position. For each of these authors, the answers to the questions posed have been different, but ultimately the questioning and the journey to the answers have unanimously been more important than either the question *or* the answer.

NOTES

1. While most of Hill's works deal in some way with this idea, for a more in-depth look, see Hill's article "Religion and the Results of the Civil War," in *Religion and the American Civil War,* ed. Randall M. Miller, Harry S. Stout, and Charles Reagan Wilson (New York: Oxford UP, 1998), 360–85. As well, see Wilson's studies about the religion of "the Lost Cause," particularly *Baptized in Blood: the Religion of the Lost Cause 1865–1920* (Athens: U Georgia P, 1983), and his longer study of southern religious faiths, *Judgment & Grace in Dixie: Southern Faiths from Faulkner to Elvis* (Athens: U Georgia P), 1995.

2. Tony Horwitz, "Georgia: Gone With the Window," in *Confederates in the Attic: Dispatches from the Unfinished Civil War* (New York: Pantheon, 1998). Horwitz's chapter on Georgia examines Jean Baudrillard's concepts of the simulacra through the lens of Atlanta's tourist industry, its reliance upon stereotypes of the South, and the repercussions that such retained images have for modern southerners and Americans in general.

3. Susan K. Cahn's 2007 *Sexual Reckonings: Southern Girls in a Troubling Age* studies in depth the repercussions suffered by many girls in the early to mid-twentieth-century South who were sexually active and/or adventurous. In particular, she focuses regularly on the guilt of those girls and young women who gave in to sexual desire.

4. In *Violence and the Sacred* Girard draws out mimetic desire to its natural conclusion—if two will desire the same object, so will three, four, or five hundred. Eventually people will begin imitating not only the desire of the mediator, but the antagonism and anger of the mediator until eventually general antagonism will lead to anger against a (usually innocent) common "enemy." The victim thus becomes sacred in the sense that it can both create the desire/anger and then soothe it back to peace. In speaking of the South, one can't help but think of lynching and public displays of racial violence as an end result of this very phenomenon.

5. Because the purpose of Giannone's study is to examine the role of spiritual love in O'Connor's works, Giannone also examines, to a lesser extent, the place of the body in such love. Chapter 1, "The Price of Guilt: *Wise Blood,*" is particularly useful in showing that O'Connor often ties physical, bodily suffering to the spirit—a technique shared by some of the writers under consideration, particularly Valerie Martin and Dorothy Allison.

6. Jill Conner Browne's series of Sweet Potato Queen books started in 1999 with *Sweet Potato Queens' Book of Love* and still continues. Her most recent book, *American Thighs: The Sweet Potato Queen's Guide to Preserving Your Assets,* was published in December 2008.

7. For a fuller examination of Catholics in the antebellum South, see Miller's introduction to *Catholics in the Old South: Essays on Church and Culture.* It examines both the

suspicions and acceptance of Catholics at various times in the South's history leading up to the Civil War.

8. In his work *But Now I See: The White Southern Racial Conversion Narrative,* Hobson writes, "Such an occurrence is hardly surprising when one considers that conversion, in a purely religious sense, has been so much a part of the life of the Calvinist South" (2).

9. In his book chronicling the lives of women in the Civil War South, *Civil Wars: Women and the Crisis of Southern Nationalism,* George C. Rable explains that, during and after the war, "church work seemed to offer women power on the one hand while reinforcing their powerlessness on the other. For example, even though in sheer numbers, women dominated the evangelical churches, men controlled discipline in the congregations, meting out harsher punishments at church trials to wayward women than to sinful men" (14–15).

10. The "Resolution on the Place of Women in Christian Service" and the later "Resolution on Women" can be found along with all SBC resolutions at www.sbc.net/resolutions/.

11. See chapter 4, in which I discuss the place of suffering in the works of Valerie Martin.

CHAPTER TWO

1. Conrad Ostwalt, "Witches and Jesus: Lee Smith's Appalachian Religion," *Southern Literary Journal* 31.1 (1998): 126. Ostwalt, dealing more significantly with elements of and struggles between primal and traditional religion in the works of Lee Smith, examines the sexual/spiritual combination, finding in the sexual an aspect of "spirituality expressed through physical, bodily experience" (113), and believes that this primal religion will ultimately never be in concert with "traditional" religious expression and belief in the works of Smith.

2. As will be discussed later in the book, however, Christ has often been seen as both feminine and womanly because of the very trait Claire loves—his suffering.

CHAPTER THREE

1. In her essay "Jesus Christ," feminist theologian Mercy Amba Oduyoye offers that African women can relate more easily to a suffering Christ: "to the Christ who knew hunger, thirst, and homelessness" (152).

2. The fascination with Mary, the most important mother figure in religion, is a fascination shared with Daniell by Claire, the Catholic novitiate in *A Recent Martyr.* Like Daniell, Claire is also concerned with the role of motherhood in the southern woman's life, although, unlike Daniell, Claire is unable to articulate this connection between a fascination with Mary and a fear of motherhood.

3. See her essays in *Fragmentation and Redemption,* particularly "The Body of Christ in the Later Middle Ages: A Reply to Leo Steinberg," 79–118.

4. In the song, Jesus speaks to the singer, referring to him or her not only as a daughter but also as bride, as in "Hear My Voice, O daughter," the heavenly bridegroom cried; "Leave also thine own country, and come and be my Bride" (Pike 43).

CHAPTER FOUR

1. For a detailed analysis and comparison of Foucault's and Freud's thoughts on masochism, including the concept of sadomasochism as productive as opposed to repressive, see Suzanne Gearheart's "Foucault's Response to Freud: Sado-masochism and the Aestheticization of Power," *Style* 29.3 (Fall 1995): 389–403.

2. Cvetkovich also sees these fantasies as productive of a queer identity that includes her "white trash" marker. The acceptance and admiration of the watchers are certainly contrary to the ridicule and humiliation she suffers at the hands of most non-family due to her status as "trash."

3. These moments in Allison's work certainly call for further theorizing of a female or lesbian gaze, and an updating of Mulvey's work on the male gaze. While some work has been done, primarily in regards to art, on the queering of the gaze, more is definitely needed.

4. For a look at the impulses of Thanatos and Eros in this novel, see Scott McClure's essay "*A Recent Martyr:* the Masochistic Aesthetic of Valerie Martin," *Contemporary Literature* 37.3 (Fall 1996): 301–417. While I agree with the majority of McClure's conclusions on masochism in this text, I believe that Emma's death instinct is not the impulse to annihilation so much as it is the desire for union (the union that comes only at the point of or after death, hence perhaps the title "little death" for the moment of union that results in orgasm).

5. Once more, we are drawn back to the in-between and liminal spaces of Bhabha and Foucault.

CHAPTER FIVE

1. My essay "Better Than Sex: Working Out with Jesus at the Lord's Gym" appeared in the 2008 collection *Shopping for Jesus: Faith in Marketing in the USA,* edited by Dominic Janes, and deals with many of the ways that religion, like other industries, uses sex for advertising purposes and treats some of the concerns brought up in this conclusion.

WORKS CITED

Abbot, Shirley. *Womenfolks: Growing up Down South.* New Haven, CT: Ticknor & Fields, 1983.

"About Us." *Christian Women for Jesus.* Christian Women for Jesus Ministries. n.d. Web. 4 July 2008.

"About Us." *XXXChurch.com.* Fireproof Ministries. n.d. Web. 4 July 2008.

Allison, Dorothy. *Bastard Out of Carolina.* New York: Plume, 1993.

———. *Cavedweller.* New York: Dutton, 1999.

———. "Her Body, Mine, and His." Thompson 44–48.

———. *Two or Three Things I Know for Sure.* New York: Plume, 1996.

Amato, Joseph A. *Victims and Values: A History and a Theory of Suffering.* New York: Greenwood, 1990.

Amende, Kathaleen. "Better Than Sex: Working Out with Jesus in the Lord's Gym." *Shopping for Jesus: Faith in Marketing in the USA.* Ed. Dominic Janes. Washington, DC: New Academia, 2008. 112–35.

Baldwin, James. *Go Tell It on the Mountain.* 1952. New York: Bantam Dell, 2005.

Benjamin, Jessica. *The Bonds of Love: Psychoanalysis, Feminism, and the Problem of Domination.* New York: Pantheon Books, 1988.

Bhabha, Homi K. *The Location of Culture.* 1994. London: Routledge, 2004.

Bracke, Sarah. "The Self—from Restoration to Annihilation: Looking at Accounts of Young Women in the Catholic Movement." *4th European Feminist Research Conference.* 28 Sept.–1 Oct. 2000, Bologna. Web. 15 Mar, 2009.

Brestin, Dee, and Kathy Troccoli. *Falling in Love With Jesus: Abandoning Yourself to the Greatest Romance of Your Life.* Nashville: Thomas Nelson, 2002.

Butler, Judith. *Gender Trouble.* 1990. New York: Routledge, 2007.

Bynum, Caroline Walker. *Fragmentation and Redemption: Essays on Gender and the Human Body in Medieval Religion.* New York: Zone Books, 1992.

Byrd, Linda. "The Emergence of the Sacred Sexual Mother in Lee Smith's *Oral History.*" *Southern Literary Journal* 31.1 (1998): 119–42.

Cahn, Susan K. *Sexual Reckonings: Southern Girls in a Troubling Age.* Cambridge, MA: Harvard UP, 2007.

Chastain, Steve. "Jesus Loves Porn Stars." *Stupid Church People.* Stupid Church People. 24 Aug. 2005. Web. 9 July 2008.

Chopin, Kate. "Two Portraits (The Nun and the Wanton)." *A Vocation and a Voice.* Ed. Emily Toth. New York: Penguin, 1991. 45–51.

Christ, Carol P. "Feminist Theology as Post-Traditional Theology." Parsons 79–96.

Cvetkovich, Ann. "Sexual Trauma/Queer Memory: Incest, Lesbianism, and Therapeutic Culture." *GLQ* (1995): 351–77.

Daniell, Rosemary. *Confessions of a {Female} Chauvinist.* Athens, GA: Hill Street, 2001.

———. *Fatal Flowers: On Sin, Sex, and Suicide in the Deep South.* New York: Avon Books, 1980.

———. *Fort Bragg & Other Points South.* New York: Henry Holt, 1988.

———. Interview with author. 6 February 1999.

———. "Re: Interview Transcript." Message to the author. 14 Feb. 1999. E-mail.

———. *A Sexual Tour of the Deep South.* 1975. New York: Holt, Rinehart and Winston, 1984.

———. *Sleeping with Soldiers: In Search of the Macho Man.* New York: Holt, Rinehart and Winston, 1984.

———. *The Woman Who Spilled Words All over Herself: Writing and Living the Zona Rosa Way.* Winchester, MA: Faber and Faber, 1997.

"Database of Megachurches in the US." *Megachurches.* Hartford Institute for Religious Research. n.d. Web. 4 July 2008.

de Beauvoir, Simone. *The Second Sex.* Trans. H. M. Parshley. 1953. New York: Vintage, 1989.

Dillman, Caroline Matheny, ed. *Southern Women.* New York: Hemisphere, 1988.

Doyle, Jacqueline. "'These Dark Woods Yet Again': Rewriting Redemption in Lee Smith's *Saving Grace.*" *ANQ: A Quarterly Journal of Short Articles, Notes, and Reviews* 41.3 (2000): 273–89.

Eckard, Paula Gallant. *Maternal Body and Voice in Toni Morrison, Bobbie Ann Mason, and Lee Smith.* Columbia: U Missouri P, 2002.

Evans, Augusta Jane. *Macaria: Or, Alters of Sacrifice.* 1864. Richmond: West & Johnston. *Project Gutenberg.* Web. 9 June 2009.

———. *St. Elmo.* 1896. Tuscaloosa: U Alabama P, 1992.

Evdokimov, Paul. *Woman and the Salvation of the World: A Christian Anthropology on the Charisms of Women.* Trans. Anthony P. Gythiel. Crestwood, NY: St. Vladimir's Seminary P, 1994.

Fennel, Valerie. "Women in Congregations." White and White, *Religion* 140–48.

Fischer, John Irwin. "Masochists, Martyrs (and Mermaids) in the Fictions of Valerie Martin." *Southern Review* 24.2 (1988): 445–50.

Foucault, Michel. "Of Other Spaces." Trans. Jay Miskowiec. *Diacritics* 16.1 (1986): 22–27. *JSTOR.* Web. 15 May 2008.

Fowler, Connie May. *Before Women Had Wings*. New York: Fawcett Columbine, 1997.

———. *The Problem with Murmur Lee*. 2005. New York: Broadway Books, 2006.

———.*When Katie Wakes: A Memoir*. New York: Doubleday, 2002. Amazon Kindle e-book file.

Fox, Thomas C. *Sexuality and Catholicism*. New York: George Braziller, 1995.

Freud, Sigmund. "The Economic Problem of Masochism." Trans. James Strachey. *The Standard Edition of the Complete Psychological Works of Sigmund Freud*. London: Hogarth, 1961. Vol. 19: 159–70.

———. *Three Essays on the Theory of Sexuality*, Trans. James Strachey. New York: Basic Books, 1962.

Friedman, Jean E. "Women's History and the Revision of Southern History." *Sex, Race, and the Role of Women in the South: Essays by Jean E. Friedman, et al.* Ed. Johanna Hawks and Sheila Skemp. Jackson: UP Mississippi, 1983. 3–12.

Gaffney, Karen. "'Excavated from the Inside': White Trash and Dorothy Allison's *Cavedweller*." *Modern Language Studies* 32.1 (2002): 43–57.

Gearheart, Suzanne. "Foucault's Response to Freud: Sado-masochism and the Aestheticization of Power." *Style* 29.3 (1995): 389–403.

Genovese, Elizabeth Fox. "Religion, Meaning and Identity in Women's Writing." *Common Knowledge* 14.1 (2008): 16–28.

Giannone, Richard. *Flannery O'Connor and the Mysteries of Love*. Champaign: U Illinois P, 1988.

Girard, Rene. *Deceit, Desire, & the Novel: Self and Other in Literary Structures*, 4th ed. Trans. Yvonne Freccero. 1961. Baltimore: Johns Hopkins UP, 1988.

———. *Violence and the Sacred*. Trans. Patrick Gregory. Baltimore: Johns Hopkins UP, 1977.

Glucklich, Ariel. *Sacred Pain: Hurting the Body for the Sake of the Soul*. Oxford, UK: Oxford UP, 2001.

Grimm, Jacob, and Wilhelm Grimm. *Household Tales*. Trans. Margaret Hunt. London: George Bell, 1884. Amazon Kindle e-book file.

Gwin, Minrose. "Nonfelicitous Space and Survivor Discourse: Reading the Incest Story in Southern Women's Fiction." *Haunted Bodies: Gender and Southern Texts*. Ed. Anne Goodwyn Jones and Susan V. Donaldson. Charlottesville: UP Virginia, 1997. 416–37.

Hansen, Ron. *Mariette in Ecstasy*. New York: Harper Perennial, 1992.

Havird, David. "The Saving Rape: Flannery O'Connor and Patriarchal Religion." *Mississippi Quarterly* 47.1 (1993). *Expanded Academic ASAP*. Web. 12 Jan 2009.

Hawks, Joanne V. "Heirs of the Southern Progressive Tradition: Women in Southern Legislatures in the 1920s." Dillman 81–102.

Henninger, Katherine. "Claiming Access: Controlling Images in Dorothy Allison." *American Quarterly* 60.3 (2004): 83–108.

Hill, Samuel S. "Religion and the Results of the Civil War." *Religion and the American Civil War.* Ed. Randall M. Miller, Harry S. Stout, and Charles Reagan Wilson. New York: Oxford UP, 1998. 360–85.

———, with Edgar T. Thompson, Anne Firor Scott, Charles Hudson, and Edwin S. Gaustad. *Religion and the Solid South.* Nashville: Abingdon, 1972.

Hobson, Fred. *But Now I See: The White Southern Racial Conversion Narrative.* Baton Rouge: Louisiana State UP, 1999.

Horvitz, Deborah. "'Sadism Demands a Story': Oedipus, Feminism, and Sexuality in Gayl Jones's *Corregidora* and Dorothy Allison's *Bastard Out of Carolina.*" *Contemporary Literature* 39.2 (1998): 238–62.

Horwitz, Tony. "Georgia: Gone With the Window." In *Confederates in the Attic: Dispatches from the Unfinished Civil War.* New York: Pantheon, 1998.

Irving, Katrina. "'Writing It Down So That It Would Be Real': Narrative Strategies in Dorothy Allison's *Bastard Out of Carolina.*" *College Literature* 25.2 (1998): 94–107.

Jones, Anne Goodwyn. *Tomorrow Is Another Day: The Woman Writer in the South, 1859–1936.* Baton Rouge: Louisiana State UP, 1981.

Kenkel, William F., and Sarah M. Shoffner. "And the Girls Became Women: Aspirations and Expectations Versus Attainments of Low-Income Black and White Southern Females." Dillman 161–76.

Ketchin, Susan. *The Christ-Haunted Landscape: Faith and Doubt in Southern Fiction.* Jackson: UP Mississippi, 1994.

Kunkel, Francis. *Passion and the Passion: Sex and Religion in Modern Literature.* Philadelphia: Westminster, 1975.

Lacan, Jacques. *The Language of the Self: The Function of Language in Psychoanalysis.* Baltimore: Johns Hopkins P, 1968.

Lewis, Sinclair. *Elmer Gantry.* 1927. New York: New American Library, 1970. Amazon Kindle e-book file.

Lynxwiler, John, and Michele Wilson. "The Code of the New Southern Belle: Generating Typifications to Structure Social Interaction." Dillman 112–26.

Martin, Valerie. *A Recent Martyr.* Baton Rouge: Louisiana State UP, 1987.

———. *Set in Motion.* 1978. New York: Washington Square Books, 1991.

———. "Surface Calm." *Love.* Spokane: Lost Horse, 1999.

———. "The Woman Who Was Never Satisfied." *The Consolation of Nature and Other Stories.* New York: Vintage Books, 1989.

Matthews, Holly F., ed. *Women in the South: An Anthropological Perspective.* Southern Anthropological Society Proceedings, no. 22. Athens: U Georgia P, 1989.

McClure, Scott. "'A Recent Martyr': The Masochistic Aesthetic of Valerie Martin." *Contemporary Literature.* 37.3 (1996): 391–417.

McCay, Mary. "An Interview with Valerie Martin." *New Orleans Review* 21.1 (1995): 6–24.

Miller, Randall M., and Jon L. Wakelyn, eds. *Catholics in the Old South: Essays on Church and Culture.* Macon, GA: Mercer UP, 1983.

Morris, David B. *The Culture of Pain.* 1991. Berkeley: U California P, 1993.

Mulvey, Laura. *Visual and Other Pleasures.* Bloomington: Indiana UP, 1989.

Nygren, Anders. "Agape and Eros." *Eros, Agape, and Philia: Readings in the Philosophy of Love.* Ed. Alan Soble. New York: Paragon House, 1989. 85–96.

O'Connor, Flannery. *Wise Blood. 3 By Flannery O'Connor.* New York: Signet, 1964.

Oduyoye, Mercy Amba. "Jesus Christ." Parsons 151–70.

O'Neill, Eugene. *Long Day's Journey into Night.* London: Jonathan Cape, 1956.

Ostwalt, Conrad. "Witches and Jesus: Lee Smith's Appalachian Religion." *Southern Literary Journal* 31.1 (1998): 98–118.

Ownby, Ted. *Subduing Satan: Religion, Recreation, & Manhood in the Rural South, 1865–1920.* Chapel Hill: U North Carolina P, 1990.

Parsons, Susan Frank, ed. *The Cambridge Companion to Feminist Theology.* Cambridge, UK: Cambridge UP, 2002.

Pasulka, Diana. "Purgatory in the Carolinas: Catholic Devotionalism in Nineteenth-Century South Carolina." *Southern Crossroads: Perspectives on Religion and Culture.* Ed. Walter H. Conser Jr. and Rodger M. Payne. Lexington: UP Kentucky, 2008. 275–302.

Pevey, Carolyn, Christine L. Williams, and Christopher G. Ellison. "Male God Imagery and Female Submission: Lessons from a Southern Baptist Ladies' Bible Class." *Qualitative Sociology* 19.1 (1996): 173–93.

Pike, Nelson. *Mystic Union: An Essay in the Phenomenology of Mysticism.* Ithaca: Cornell UP, 1992.

Portillo, Tina. "I Get Real: Celebrating my Sadomasochistic Soul." Thompson 49–55.

Pui-Lan, Kwok. "Feminist Theology as Intercultural Discourse." Parsons 23–39.

Rable, George C. *Civil Wars: Women and the Crisis of Southern Nationalism.* Urbana: U Illinois P, 1989.

Rambuss, Richard. *Closet Devotions.* Durham, NC: Duke UP, 1998.

"Resolutions." *Resolution on the Place of Women in Christian Service.* Southern Baptist Convention, n.d. Web. 4 Feb. 2008.

Reynolds, Sheri. *Bitterroot Landing.* 1994. New York, Berkley Books, 1997.

———. *The Rapture of Canaan.* 1996. New York: Berkley Books, 1997.

Richardson, Miles. "Speaking and Hearing (in Contrast to Touching and Seeing) the Sacred." White, *Religion* 13–22.

Riser-Smith, Emily. "Kate Chopin as Modernist: A Reading of 'Lilacs' and 'Two Portraits,'" *Domestic Goddesses*. Ed. Kim Wells. Web. 14 July 2009.

Romine, Scott. *The Narrative Forms of Southern Community*. Baton Rouge: Louisiana State UP, 1999.

Ross, Susan A. "Church and Sacrament—Community and Worship." Parsons 224–42.

Ruether, Rosemary Radford. "The Emergence of Christian Feminist Theology." Parsons 3–22.

Scott, Anne Firor. *The Southern Lady: From Pedestal to Politics 1830–1930*. 1970. Charlottesville: UP Virginia, 1995.

Sims, Patsy. *Can Somebody Shout Amen!* New York: St. Martin's, 1988.

Sizer, Sandra. *Gospel Hymns and Social Religion: The Rhetoric of Nineteenth-Century Revivalism*. Philadelphia: Temple UP, 1978.

Slee, Nicola. "The Holy Spirit and Spirituality." Parsons 171–89.

Smith, Lee. *Black Mountain Breakdown*. New York: Ballantine Books, 1980.

———. *Conversations with Lee Smith*. By Linda Tate. Jackson: UP Mississippi, 2001.

———. *The Devil's Dream*. New York: Ballantine, 1992.

———. *Fair and Tender Ladies*. 1988. New York: Ballantine, 2003.

———. *Family Linen*, New York: Ballantine, 1985.

———. *The Last Day the Dogbushes Bloomed*. 1968. Baton Rouge: Louisiana State UP, 1994.

———. *Oral History*. 1983. Rpt. New York: Ballantine, 2003.

———. *Saving Grace*. New York: Ballantine, 1995.

———. "Tongues of Fire." *Me and My Baby View the Eclipse: Stories*. New York: Ballantine, 1990.

Smith, Lillian. *Killers of the Dream*. New York: W. W. Norton, 1949.

Smith, Rebecca. *Gender Dynamics in the Fiction of Lee Smith: Examining Language and Narrative Strategies*. San Francisco: International Scholars Publications, 1997.

Smith, Rob. "An Interview with Valerie Martin." *Contemporary Literature* 34.1 (1993): 1–18.

Smith-Riser, Emily. "Kate Chopin as Modernist: A Reading of 'Lilacs' and 'Two Portraits.'" *Domestic Goddesses*. Ed. Kim Wells. August 23, 1999. Web. 18 Oct. 2009.

Steinberg, Leo. *The Sexuality of Christ in Renaissance Art and in Modern Oblivion*, 2nd ed. Chicago: U Chicago P, 1997.

Tamke, Susan. *Make a Joyful Noise Unto the Lord: Hymns as a Reflection of Victorian Social Attitudes*. Athens: Ohio UP, 1978.

Thompson, Mark, ed. *Leatherfolk: Radical Sex, People, Politics and Practice*. Los Angeles: Daedalus, 2004.

Thumma, Scott Lee. "Rising Out of the Ashes: An Exploration of One Congregation's Use of Southern Symbolism." White, *Religion* 149–58.

Tillich, Paul. *Dynamics of Faith.* 1957. New York: Harper Perennial, 2001.

Uebel, Michael. "Masochism in America." *American Literary History* 14.2 (2002): 389–411.

Underhill, Evelyn. *The Essentials of Mysticism.* 1995. Oxford, UK: Oneworld, 1999.

United Methodist Hymnal. Nashville: Abingdon P, 1989.

Vidler, Anthony. *The Architectural Uncanny: Essays in Modern Unhomely.* Boston: MIT P, 1992.

Warren, George W. *Hymns and Tunes as Sung at St. Thomas's Church New York.* New York: Harper & Brothers, 1888.

Weber, Alison. *Teresa of Avila and the Rhetoric of Femininity.* Princeton, NJ: Princeton UP, 1990.

White, Chris. "(Not) Dying of Shame: Female Sexual Submission in 1890s' Erotica." *Critical Survey* 15.3 (2003): 74–91.

White, Deborah Gray. *Ar'n't I a Woman? Female Slaves in the Plantation South.* Rev. ed. New York: W. W. Norton, 1999.

White, O. Kendall, Jr. and Daryl White. *Religion in the Contemporary South: Diversity, Community, and Identity.* Southern Anthropological Society Proceedings, no. 28. Athens: U Georgia P, 1995.

Wilson, Charles Reagan. *Baptized in Blood: The Religion of the Lost Cause 1865–1920.* Athens: U Georgia P, 1983.

———. *Judgment & Grace in Dixie: Southern Faiths from Faulkner to Elvis.* Athens: U Georgia P, 1995.

Wolfe, Margaret Ripley. *Daughters of Canaan: A Saga of Southern Women.* Lexington: UP Kentucky, 1995.

Wolkomir, Michelle. "'GIVING IT UP TO GOD': Negotiating Femininity in Support Groups for Wives of Ex-Gay Christian Men." *Gender & Society* 18.6 (2004): 735–55.

INDEX